The Iditarod

ALASKA GEOGRAPHIC® / Volume 28, Number 4 / 2001

To teach many more to better know and more wisely use our natural resources...

EDITOR
Penny Rennick

PRODUCTION DIRECTOR
Kathy Doogan

ASSOCIATE EDITOR
Susan Beeman

MARKETING DIRECTOR
Mark Weber

ADMINISTRATIVE ASSISTANT
Camille Oliver

ISBN: 1-56661-057-5

PRICE TO NON-MEMBERS THIS ISSUE: $23.95

PRINTED IN U.S.A.

POSTMASTER
Send address changes to:

ALASKA GEOGRAPHIC®
P.O. Box 93370, Anchorage, Alaska 99509-3370

COVER: *Thousands of dogs and humans have traveled the Iditarod National Historic Trail, from its creation as a gold rush track in the early 1900s to its modern use as a race route. (Jeff Schultz/Alaska Stock)*

PREVIOUS PAGE: *Moonlight and stars illuminate teams resting at Rainy Pass, the first checkpoint in the Alaska Range and 224 miles from the starting line. (Jeff Schultz/Alaska Stock)*

FACING PAGE: *Three-time champion Jeff King of Denali Park shares the glory of the winner's seat with lead dogs Jenna and Red. Mushers emphasize that dogs are the true athletes of the Iditarod Trail Sled Dog Race. (Jeff Schultz/Alaska Stock)*

ALASKA GEOGRAPHIC® (ISSN 0361-1353) is published quarterly by The Alaska Geographic Society, 639 West International Airport Rd. #38, Anchorage, AK 99518. Periodicals postage paid at Anchorage, Alaska, and additional mailing offices. Copyright © 2001 The Alaska Geographic Society. All rights reserved. Registered trademark: Alaska Geographic, ISSN 0361-1353; key title Alaska Geographic. This issue published December 2001.

THE ALASKA GEOGRAPHIC SOCIETY is a non-profit, educational organization dedicated to improving geographic understanding of Alaska and the North, putting geography back in the classroom, and exploring new methods of teaching and learning.

ABOUT THIS ISSUE

Associate Editor Susan Beeman wrote the text for this issue except where noted. The editors would like to thank Iditarod Trail Committee Race Director Joanne Potts and Development Director Greg Bill for their time and patience in answering questions and reviewing text; ITC Volunteer Coordinator Cheryl Church for information about volunteers; Official Iditarod Photographer Jeff Schultz for his excellent photos and wealth of Iditarod knowledge; Jerry Austin, Dave Monson, Dick Mackey, Rick Mackey, Emmitt Peters, Libby Riddles, Martin Buser, Jeff King, Doug Swingley, Vi Redington, Joe Delia, Bob Sept, Jim Lanier, Anna Bondarenko, Joe Pendergrass, Bill Mayer, Bill Devine, Christine Kriger, Leo Rasmussen, Mike Zaidlicz, Dave Stimson for granting interviews; Lana Creer-Harris for help with photos; Bruce Merrell and Dan Flemming for research help; and the Bureau of Land Management, Office of Public Affairs, for printed material on the history of the Iditarod Trail. ∎

MEMBERS RECEIVE ALASKA GEOGRAPHIC®, a high-quality, colorful quarterly that devotes each issue to monographic, in-depth coverage of a specific northern region or resource-oriented subject. Back issues are also available (see page 96). Membership is $49 ($59 to non-U.S. addresses) per year. To order or to request a free catalog of back issues, contact: Alaska Geographic Society, P.O. Box 93370, Anchorage, AK 99509-3370; phone (907) 562-0164 or toll free (888) 255-6697, fax (907) 562-0479, e-mail: akgeo@akgeo.com. A complete list of our back issues, maps and other products can also be found on our web site at www.akgeo.com.

SUBMITTING PHOTOGRAPHS: Those interested in submitting photos for possible publication should write or refer to our website for a list of upcoming topics or other photo needs and a copy of our editorial guidelines. We cannot be responsible for unsolicited submissions. Please note that submissions must be accompanied by sufficient postage for return by priority mail plus delivery confirmation.

CHANGE OF ADDRESS: When you move, the post office may not automatically forward your ALASKA GEOGRAPHIC®. To ensure continuous service, please notify us at least six weeks before moving. Send your new address and membership number or a mailing label from a recent issue of ALASKA GEOGRAPHIC® to: Address Change, Alaska Geographic Society, P.O. Box 93370, Anchorage, AK 99509-3370.

If your issue is returned to us by the post office because it is undeliverable, we will contact you to ask if you wish to receive a replacement for a small fee to cover the cost of additional postage to reship the issue.

COLOR SEPARATIONS: **Graphic Chromatics**
PRINTING: **Banta Publications Group / Hart Press**

Contents

Introduction

On the first Saturday of every March, at the starting line of the Iditarod Trail Sled Dog Race, downtown Anchorage swells with people and dogs. Veteran and rookie mushers, hundreds of yipping huskies, and thousands of race fans gather, the official countdown booming over them on Fourth Avenue.

"Five-four-three-two-one-GO!"

The spectators cheer, drowning out their mitten-muffled applause. Another team has begun the uncertain days and nights of the famous race from Anchorage to Nome.

For many people, the word "Iditarod" brings to mind the modern race: sled dogs barking at the starting line, mushers bundled in parkas against the wind and winter cold, mountains and frozen coastline, auroral nights with only the whisper

of dog feet and the sled's runners moving along the trail. The Iditarod National Historic Trail, home to the Iditarod Trail Sled Dog Race, also encompasses a history rich in early exploration, gold discoveries, and pioneer footsteps across nearly 1,000 miles of Alaska's wilderness. This book brings to life the trail's history and celebrates the race's 30th anniversary in 2002.

Commonly said to be 1,049 miles, the Iditarod is actually a series of trails that varies in length, depending on the route taken. The race alternates between a northern route in even years and a southern route in odd, from Anchorage to Nome; at about 1,100 miles each, they are longer than the historical route. Race officials adopted the 1,049 figure as a symbolic distance, rounding the number down and

echoing Alaska's induction as the nation's 49th state. While Anchorage and Nome are only 537 air miles apart, traveling the Iditarod Trail can be compared in length to going overland between Denver and Los Angeles or Minneapolis and Washington, D.C. The race route loosely follows the historic route, passing through many of the same remote villages.

The Iditarod Trail originated in the same way as many modern transportation corridors — from game trails. From Alaska's Native people hunting animals, to explorers and missionaries in search of furs and converts, to miners seeking their fortune in goldfields and creek bottoms, thousands of feet have trod the famous course. Today's sled dog race reflects the determination of 20 men in 1925 who delivered, via dog team relay, a package of diphtheria serum to Nome, using part of the same trail, after an outbreak of the disease erupted among the town's people. For prospectors, gold rush mail carriers, and adventure seekers, the Iditarod Trail has always been a place to test one's survival skills and face Alaska on its own terms.

FACING PAGE: *Open year-round, the Iditarod Trail Race Headquarters in Wasilla, 40 miles north of Anchorage, presents visitors with Iditarod Trail history and tidbits about today's sled dog race. Musher portraits, videos, information packets, and merchandise are available inside, and during summer, Raymie Redington offers sled dog rides nearby in a wheeled cart on a dirt trail through the forest. (Susan Beeman, AGS staff)*

IDITAROD TRAIL RACE
〜 RACE 〜
HEADQUARTERS • WASILLA ALASKA

THE IDITAROD TRAIL

IT IS A NATIONAL HISTORIC TRAIL, SO DESIGNATED BY THE CONGRESS OF THE UNITED STATES, FROM SEWARD ON THE SOUTH CENTRAL COAST TO NOME ON THE BERING SEA. IT WAS A HIGHWAY, A MAIL ROUTE, A GOLD AVENUE FROM THE INTERIOR. PART OF IT BECAME A LIFELINE FOR DIPTHERIA SERUM TO BE CARRIED TO NOME DURING THE EPIDEMIC OF 1925.

IT IS NOW A TRAPPERS' TRAIL, A RECREATION TRAIL, STILL A "LIFELINE" FOR SOME VILLAGES, AND THE AVENUE FOR THE MOST CHALLENGING AND DEMANDING LONG DISTANCE SLED DOG RACE IN THE WORLD... "THE IDITAROD", 1049 MILES, ANCHORAGE TO NOME, THROUGH ALASKA'S WILDERNESS, OVER MOUNTAIN PASSES, DOWN FROZEN RIVERS, AND ALONG THE WIND SWEPT SEA COAST. TRULY THE MAJESTY AND MYSTERY THAT IS "THE LAST GREAT RACE ON EARTH".

DONATED BY
EXON
Young
SIGNS

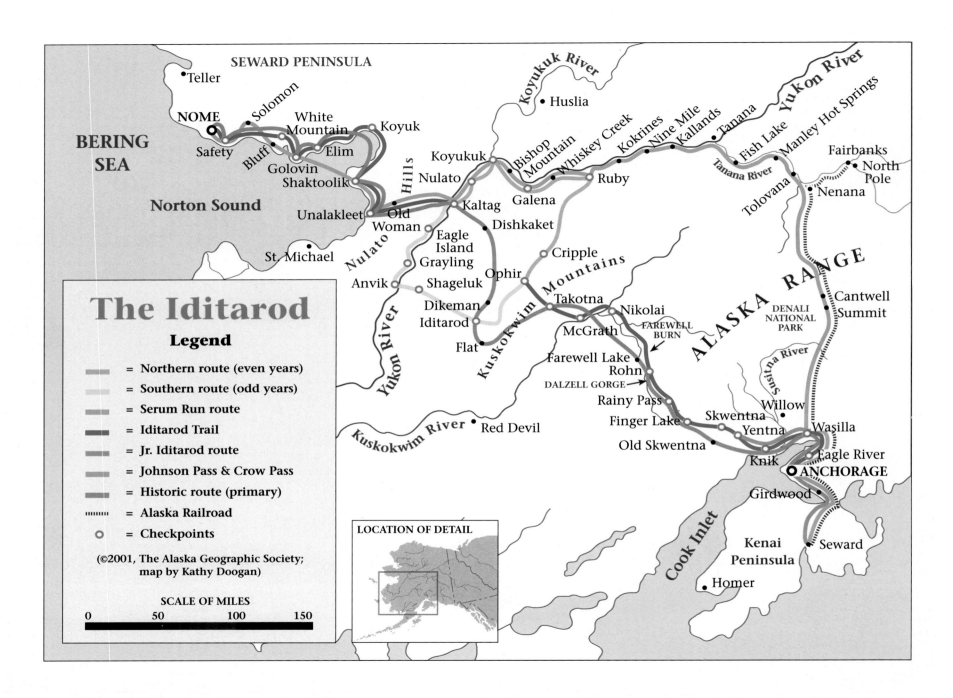

The Iditarod

Legend

- ▬▬ = Northern route (even years)
- ▬▬ = Southern route (odd years)
- ▬▬ = Serum Run route
- ▬▬ = Iditarod Trail
- ▬▬ = Jr. Iditarod route
- ▬▬ = Johnson Pass & Crow Pass
- ▬▬ = Historic route (primary)
- ┅┅┅ = Alaska Railroad
- ○ = Checkpoints

(©2001, The Alaska Geographic Society;
map by Kathy Doogan)

SCALE OF MILES

0   50   100   150

LOCATION OF DETAIL

SEWARD PENINSULA
Teller
Solomon
NOME
White Mountain
Koyuk
Safety
Bluff
Elim
Golovin
Shaktoolik
BERING SEA
Norton Sound
Unalakleet
Old Woman
St. Michael
Anvik
Nulato Hills
Yukon River
Dikeman
Iditarod
Flat
Shageluk
Grayling
Eagle Island
Ophir
Cripple
Dishkaket
Kaltag
Nulato
Koyukuk
Galena
Ruby
Bishop Mountain
Whiskey Creek
Kokrines
Nine Mile
Kallands
Tanana
Fish Lake
Manley Hot Springs
Huslia
Koyukuk River
Yukon River
Tanana River
Tolovana
Fairbanks
North Pole
Nenana
Kuskokwim Mountains
Takotna
Nikolai
McGrath
Farewell Lake
Rohn
FAREWELL BURN
DALZELL GORGE
Rainy Pass
Finger Lake
Old Skwentna
Kuskokwim River
Red Devil
Skwentna
Yentna
Susitna River
Willow
Wasilla
Knik
Eagle River
ANCHORAGE
Girdwood
ALASKA RANGE
DENALI NATIONAL PARK
Cantwell
Summit
Cook Inlet
Kenai Peninsula
Homer
Seward

k Swenson is the only five-time Iditarod
...ner. His lead dog Andy, right, led the
...sher's teams to victory four times and lived
...ost 20 years. After his death, Andy was
...ffed and is on display at Iditarod
...adquarters. Swenson's son is named after
... canine champ. (Bill Devine)

...the trail regularly during summer.
...ikers traverse Crow Pass, a part of the
...ail between Girdwood and Eagle River,
...ear Anchorage; every July, contestants
...n a footrace over this terrain in the
...Crow Pass Crossing." Walking the Bering
...ea shoreline east of Nome is another
...ay to explore the trail during snow-
...ree months. But for those in search of
...utdoor challenge and media coverage,
...he Iditarod Trail Sled Dog Race kicks off
...rom downtown Anchorage every year,
...ringing thousands of spectators to
...railside to watch and encourage their
...avorite mushers. Other races, such as the
...r. Iditarod, Iditasport, and Iron Dog also
...it the stamina and skill of boys, girls,
...en, and women against often harsh
...conditions on this time-honored trail.

The Iditarod Trail cuts across federal,
...state, municipal, private, and Native
Corporation lands, creating a management challenge for all involved. Now
under Bureau of Land Management
(BLM) control, it's also administered by
the Iditarod National Historic Trail
Advisory Council, a group representing
the Secretaries of Interior and Agriculture,
Governor of Alaska, and private land
managers and users. Another group, the
Iditarod Trail Blazers, provides volunteer
trail maintenance and construction help.

Many modern mushers consider the
dogs the true athletes in the Iditarod Trail
Sled Dog Race. Since the first race from
Anchorage to Nome in 1973, the Iditarod
Trail Committee (ITC) has created and
amended rules about dog care, required
equipment, musher qualifications, and
trail etiquette, transforming what began
as a three-week "camping trip" into an
organized event that draws high-caliber
competitors and international attention.

Nearly 100 years ago, when a U.S.
Army survey crew blazed and measured
what was to be the Seward to Nome
Mail Trail, it took them more than two
months. Today's front-runners, following
nearly the same route, reach Nome in
scarcely more than one week. Here is the
story of the Iditarod National Historic
Trail and the Iditarod Trail Sled Dog
Race. Hop aboard the sled runners and
take a ride on the Iditarod. ■

History of the Iditarod Trail

Long before outdoor enthusiasts and modern equipment created trailheads and cut roads through Alaska's wilderness, animals walked the forests and tundra, leaving behind hoof and paw prints. Regular use of favored routes wore grooves into the spongy mosses, mucky creek bottoms, and alpine soils. Alaska Natives in search of hides and fur for clothing and fresh meat for food followed these game trails in a seasonal quest for survival, creating wider, more substantial trails. In winter, Natives hooked dog teams to sleds and hunted and hauled their bounty home with the help of canine power. These summer footpaths and winter sled trails were the genesis of today's Iditarod National Historic Trail.

Geography of the Trail

The primary route of the historical Iditarod Trail crosses forest, mountain, bog, and tundra. Its southern section, from Seward to Eagle River, winds through steep mountain passes covered in hemlock, spruce, and birch forests. Eagle River's foothills roll down to meet Knik Arm's mudflats. An expanse of mixed forests and wetlands continues to Old Skwentna; the trail then crosses the braided Susitna River, a major South-central Alaska waterway. Past the river it climbs into the Alaska Range, topping out at 3,160-foot Rainy Pass. From there down the north side of the range, the mountainous surroundings turn to gentle slopes of tundra, brush and

Winter temperatures in Alaska's Interior routinely fall to minus 60 degrees Fahrenheit. This photo was taken at Farewell Lake in 1974, near the remains of French Joe's establishment. Rumor has it that he kept a faulty thermometer, permanently stuck in the subzero range, outside his roadhouse to encourage visitors to stay longer; for him it meant more income. (Marydith Beeman)

explorers through regions the locals knew well.

When Russian explorers began arriving on Alaska's coasts in the mid 1700s, they put existing trails to use, but hiking and hauling freight through boggy terrain was nearly impossible during summer, and they tended to scout via boat on rivers rather than by land. Russian Lt. L.A. Zagoskin said in the early 1840s of Nulato, an Athabaskan village east of Norton Sound and today an Iditarod Trail Sled Dog Race checkpoint, "The level land has many small lakes and basins in which the heaping water from melted snow is held all summer."

Following Alaska's purchase from Russia in 1867, the U.S. government sent expeditions into the wilderness to take stock of the country's new acquisition, but the surveys were generally under-funded and the crews too small. The government was unwilling to invest much in such a sparsely populated place they knew so little about. Explorations

A Stroke of Luck

Many prospectors had come to Alaska unprepared for the harsh conditions; some dropped cumbersome supplies beside the trails, only to find food stocks in settlements too low to sustain them through the long winter. Partly in response, the military sent out their own teams of trailblazers in search of efficient routes to the goldfields but weren't always successful either.

Anthropologist William S. Schneider, in *Interior Alaska: A Journey Through Time* (1986) writes that Lt. Joseph Herron and his party "left from Cook Inlet in late summer of 1899, ascended the Susitna River to the Yentna, thence to the Kichatna, across Simpson Pass [12 miles northeast of Rainy Pass] in the Alaska Range and onto the upper Kuskokwim River…. Herron hoped to find a practical all-American route to the Yukon [River], but the party was terribly overloaded and depended on horses, which were totally inappropriate for the brushy terrain and swift stream crossings. With 15 horses and eight men, they carried 3,300 pounds of gear and supplies, including 600 pounds of bacon and 1,000 pounds of flour. Finally they became bogged down in the upper Kuskokwim lowlands, so they abandoned the horses and cached many of their supplies, including some bacon.

"Lost, and with the season rapidly advancing, they were in a desperate situation. Fortunately they hadn't gone far when a bear broke into the cache and ate the bacon. Unbeknown to Herron, Chief Sesui and the other Telida Indians [Telida is about 40 miles northwest of Nikolai] were hunting in the area and happened to kill the same bear that had found the soldiers' bacon. When they butchered the animal, Sesui recognized the white man's food in its stomach and knew there must be strangers nearby. He backtracked the bear's trail to Herron's cache, then followed the distinctive horseshoe and white man's boot tracks until he reached them.

"…Chief Sesui…took them to Telida and equipped them with mitts, caps, moccasins, and snowshoes…. After a couple of months, when there was enough snow for traveling, the Indians guided the soldiers…to Tanana Village on the Yukon." ◼

by non-Natives to Alaska's Interior had been, up until the mid 1800s, virtually nonexistent, and even though by the late 1800s U.S. military expeditions had successfully traveled from Prince William Sound through Canada to the Interior, these routes were long and circuitous; men dreamed of a shorter, more direct route across Alaska, one that did not cross Canadian land.

Chasing the Gold

Discovery of gold in Alaska from 1880 to a few years after the turn of the century attracted thousands of newcomers who established year-round mining camps. Full-fledged towns sprang up quickly in what had been wilderness for millennia. The need grew for delivery of supplies and for a system of communicating with family members back home. Sacks of mail began arriving along with food, dry goods, and tools, pulled by teams of strong, hardy, mixed-breed dogs; some of the main trails doubled as wagon roads in summer and sled trails in winter, but remained isolated segments or merely side trails from towns served by steamboats.

By the early 1900s, a series of trails connected the ice-free port of Seward with the Innoko River region, and with Kaltag, on the lower Yukon River. An overland mail route existed from Kaltag to Nome, though most mail in and out of the Innoko region still moved via the Yukon, by boat in summer and dog team in winter.

The Alaska Central Railway, a poorly funded enterprise begun by a group of Seattle businessmen in an effort to cut a

ABOVE: *In 1910, Walter L. Goodwin and a crew of men surveyed the "Seward to Nome Mail Trail" for the Alaska Road Commission. The wheel pictured is a cyclometer, a measuring device used to record the distance traveled, nearly 1,000 miles by dog team. (Courtesy of Bureau of Land Management)*

RIGHT: *Without Joe and Vi Redington, the Iditarod Trail's history would have lain dormant. After coming to Alaska in 1948 and marrying, the couple devoted their lives to restoring and preserving the trail that ran through woods near their Knik homestead. (Jeff Schultz/Alaska Stock)*

path from Resurrection Bay to the Tanana River and the goldfields near Fairbanks, began laying track north from Seward in 1903. Struggling financially, the company changed hands, and the new owners searched for outside funding. Gerrit A.A. Middelberg, a retired Dutch railway engineer, came to Alaska in 1905 at the request of Dutch financier Salomon Frederick van Oss to assess the possibility of investing in the Alaska Central. Middelberg's notes from his outing along the trail read, "By train at first, then on foot for some hours, and the rest on horseback.... We slept in a log cabin, all eight of us, with five dogs.... On horseback and on foot past precipices, over glaciers, all most beautiful...." Though the rawness and grandeur of Alaska were not lost on Middelberg, van Oss decided not to invest. Alaska Central reorganized in 1909 into the Alaska Northern Railway Company, and railway construction from Seward continued, but still at a snail's pace due to lack of funds.

Despite the railroad tracks stopping abruptly, miners and mail carriers continued to follow the route north from Seward, some on their way to Fairbanks, but most heading for the Innoko area.

Traffic and precious cargo—gold—also moved south from the Interior to Seward, then to Seattle and San Francisco. The majority of travelers were men, but women and children accompanied some parties.

In late January of 1908, the U.S. Army's Alaska Road Commission sent Walter L. Goodwin and a crew of three men to survey the winter route, not yet known as the Iditarod Trail. Officials believed it was the shortest course from Seward to Nome. If the Army couldn't stop miners from getting lost and injured, they could at least help them find their way.

On foot, the survey party followed the existing railbed north from Seward to Kern Creek, near Girdwood, then cleared and marked the rest of the trail to Knik, through the Alaska Range, and all the way to Kaltag by March 15, where they "had the coldest weather of the entire trip...43 degrees below zero." On April 5, 1908, the men reached Nome, 66 days after leaving Seward. They'd walked nearly 1,000 miles.

On Christmas day the same year, prospecting partners William Dikeman and John Beaton discovered gold just outside the town of Flat, near what some called the Haiditarod River. (Other Athabaskan names, such as Yalchikatna, Tachaichagat, and Haidilatna differed depending on who wrote them down. The word was eventually standardized to Iditarod.) Both men had come north during the Klondike gold rush, and both had gone from the Klondike to the Seward Peninsula and back to Fairbanks looking for gold. Dikeman had been in the Innoko region in 1907, but became discouraged when he'd found no room left to stake a claim on Ganes Creek, and

Mail carriers and their teams rest in Seward. Freight dogs used in the early twentieth century were larger and heavier than today's dogs that run the Iditarod Trail Sled Dog Race. A 500-pound load of mail could be pulled by seven to nine dogs, but eight to 10 were normal; annual pay for a mail driver then was $2,225. (B81.19.2, Anchorage Museum of History and Art)

Legend

—— = Dikeman and Beaton's route by boat

···· = Dikeman and Beaton's route by sled (on foot)

x = Gold discovery

Kaltag

YUKON RIVER

Innoko R.

Iditarod R.

Dishkaket

Ophir

Anvik

Dikeman

Ganes Creek

Iditarod

Otter Cr.

Flat

Discovery

KUSKOKWIM RIVER

(©2001, The Alaska Geographic Society; map by Kathy Doogan)

he'd left the area. Beaton had been in Fairbanks that year, but traveled to Ophir in 1908. The men met in Anvik and decided to pool their resources.

They bought the steamer *K.P.M.* and headed up the Innoko River in July. At the confluence of the Iditarod and Innoko Rivers, they made the fateful decision to follow the Iditarod, as it had thus far been unexplored for the coveted

Mules pull the first passenger coach on a tram built between Iditarod and Flat, eight miles apart. As hundreds of people poured into the area and the towns grew, additional infrastructure was created to accommodate new arrivals. (Courtesy of Pat Roppel)

yellow metal. The river level in summer was low, and many times Dikeman and Beaton's boat got stuck on sandbars. Each time, the men had to unload provisions from the *K.P.M.* to refloat it. The trip took longer than planned, and by the time they neared the Iditarod's headwaters, the river was beginning to ice up. The prospectors pulled their boat onto shore and began building a winter shelter.

Once the ground froze, they explored the area, crafting a sled and heading south till they reached Otter Creek. Twelve miles up that creek, Dikeman and Beaton started digging. Twelve feet down, they struck a major gold deposit. They staked claims for themselves and for a few friends, then returned to their cabin

and waited through the long winter for the river ice to melt and allow travel once again. No one else knew yet of their discovery.

When spring arrived, they steamed back down the Iditarod River and up the Innoko to the recording office at Ophir, a circuitous 520-mile journey covering hundreds more miles than would have an overland trip. Enroute, the prospectors met another boat, the *Martha Clam*, on its way from Dishkaket to Fairbanks with a load of ore. Upon that boat's arrival in Fairbanks, news of a new gold discovery in the Iditarod area spread like wildfire. When Dikeman and Beaton reached Ophir, news spread fast there too. Hope was renewed for many still seeking riches from the harsh land, and they set their sights on Dikeman and Beaton's "Discovery Cabin."

This new promise of riches brought an onslaught of arrivals to the Interior, but because of natural climate cycles and supply difficulties, large-scale mining of the area was slow. There were not enough boats to transport supplies upriver, and a lack of rain in the summer of 1909 left water levels low. Muskegs made the ground too spongy for land transportation, and many prospectors had to use small boats to ferry loads of food and gear from farther downriver than they'd expected.

Recording their new mining claims at Ophir was also an inconvenience, so in 1909, the government agreed to divide the Innoko district into two sections. The western portion became the Otter District, with its recording office at the

LEAVE	DOGS	ENTRIES	DRIVER	NO	A.M.	P.M.	P.M.	TIME
OUT 9:10	6	MATHEWSON / BOWKER	GREER	2	Bunched 3 AND 4 POSITION 12:25	1:20 3/4 2:27 1/2	1:41	WEATHER BAD 10 BELOW Z
9:00	5	GUSTUFSON	SELF	1	12:25	12:29 1/2	1:41	HEAVY NORTH WIND
9:20	7	HOWARD	SELF	3	SECOND 11:28	12:25 12:29	1:15 1/2 1:18	TRAIL HEAVY
		REVELL						SNOW DRIFTING
9:30 A.M.	5	DIXON	SELF	4	FIRST 11:28	12:14 1/2	1:09 1/2 1:30	BAD

JANUARY 20 1916

ANCHORAGE P.M.	DOGS	ENTRIES	DRIVER	NO	EAGLE RIVER 14 M.	BOARDING CARS 17 1/2 M.	PETERS CREEK 23 M.	OLD KNIK 27 M.	TOTAL TIME H. M.
5:50	6	MATHEWSON / BOWKER	GREER	2	4:38	3:31	2:30	1:41	8:40
6:00:30	5	GUSTUFSON	SELF	1	4:38	3:31	2:30	1:41	9:00:30
5:19	7	HOWARD	SELF	3	3:48	2:52	2:02	1:18	7:59
OUT		REVELL							
5:22	5	DIXON	SELF	4	4:02	3:00	2:10 1/2 2:11	1:30	7:52

McCAIN STUDIO

new settlement of Iditarod. Riverboat and steamship companies advertised the new gold discovery and encouraged travel to Iditarod. Gold seekers and their families flooded the town, making it the biggest city in the Interior for the next two years. Business people followed and the settlements — Iditarod, Flat, and Dikeman — became full-fledged towns and supply centers. Frank Stanley built Stanley's Roadhouse for miners at the confluence of Flat and Otter Creeks in June 1910, with a footbridge across Otter Creek for easy access. Banks, courts, and newspapers thrived. Between Iditarod and Flat, eight miles apart, miners built a wooden tramway to ferry supplies back and forth. No other permanent trails led out of the wetlands around Iditarod, the head of

navigation during late spring and early summer. Most traveled to the area by foot, skis, or snowshoes in winter from Seward, the "gateway to the Iditarod," and in summer by boat up the Yukon and Kuskokwim Rivers.

Jim Pitcher, one pioneer who'd worked various jobs around Alaska at the turn of the century, embodied the impulsive atmosphere of the times. He'd married Blanche Hedgpeth, a young woman who made the trip to Alaska from Oregon aboard the steamer *Alameda* in November of 1909. A few months later, while on duty for the Forest Service along the Iditarod Trail near Girdwood, Pitcher met up with his old friend Jack Stiegler, who was on his way back to a successful placer mine in the Innoko district. Pitcher

$125000.00 in Gold Bricks
Assay Office, American Bank of Alaska.
Iditarod Alaska.

ABOVE, LEFT: *By 1916, dog racing had become a popular pastime for men and women in many Alaska communities. (B63.16.71, Anchorage Museum of History and Art)*

ABOVE: *Women and men sought their fortunes in Alaska's goldfields. Mail carriers hauled gold bricks such as these, shown at Iditarod's American Bank of Alaska, to Seward for transport to banks in Seattle and San Francisco. (Courtesy of Pat Roppel)*

Nulato, Alaska.
June. 8, 1899.

ABOVE: *The U.S. Postal Service established an office in Nulato, an Athabaskan village on the Yukon River, in 1897, and by 1900, two steamboats per day were stopping to buy firewood. During even years, the Iditarod Trail Sled Dog Race follows a northern route between Ophir and Kaltag; Nulato is one of the checkpoints. (Jasper Wyman collection, #288, Anchorage Museum of History and Art)*

LEFT: *Airmail began to replace dog team delivery in the mid 1920s, and miners had ceased traveling to the Interior. The Iditarod Trail fell into disuse for almost 50 years. (B80.41.145, Anchorage Museum of History and Art)*

writes, "…I suddenly decided to go with Jack. I had with me only an extra pair of socks, but I submitted my resignation…. I also wrote a letter to my newly acquired wife, who was at the hotel in Seward, and told her to follow me to the Innoko by steamer in June. Then I was ready to hit the 450-mile-long trail to Innoko and Iditarod." Pitcher describes struggling through deep snow on snowshoes and breaking trail for their small dog team, and of the dangers of mountain travel in winter, such as breaking through the snow's crust and avalanches "so violent that the suction pulled in dozens of spruce trees, some of them a foot or more in diameter." Pitcher's wife met him at Takotna that summer, after having traveled by steamboat to Bethel, up the Kuskokwim River to McGrath, "then by canoe which overtook a horse scow and brought her to Takotna." The couple hiked 10 miles to Pitcher's waiting boat. "Blanche," he writes, "had packed two immense warbags with things she thought necessary. I remember that two flatirons and a pair of skates were included!"

Another miner, Kenneth Gideon from Minnesota, arrived in Iditarod in 1916, but by then the golden light of discovery was fading from the area. Still, cross-country travel hadn't changed, and he writes, "A snow trail, besides making travel by sled possible, is smooth under foot… consequently, the selection of suitable foot gear is a simple matter. A trip in the summer, on the other hand, involves travel over every conceivable kind of terrain, making hob-nailed boots necessary one hour and rubber-soled sneakers desirable the next, with hip boots in demand for fording streams. Creeping vines trip the summer traveler, loose rocks twist his ankle, and he slips on slime-covered creek bottoms and staggers through patches of soft sand." Even today, summer travelers opt for boat or plane transport across much of Alaska.

In November of 1910, the Alaska Road Commission again appointed Goodwin to blaze the same trail he'd followed two

A "dog team express" hauls a load down Nome's boardwalk; the dogs wear leather harnesses similar to those made for horses. Nome's Front Street welcomes finishers of today's 1,049-mile race. (Courtesy of Ethel A. Becker)

years earlier. He departed Nome with several men and six teams of seven dogs each. Crewmembers paid 50 cents per day for food from their daily wage of $3.50. They chose future roadhouse sites approximately one day's travel apart.

Rusted relics of the mining industry at Crow Creek, near Girdwood, remind modern Iditarod Trail travelers that each tool had to be transported by foot or dog team. Gold seekers on their way to Iditarod trekked from Seward over Crow Pass to Knik, where they outfitted themselves for the long journey inland. (Rich Reid)

They reached Seward on February 25, 1911, having surveyed the official Seward to Nome Mail Trail.

Racing Fever

The same year the gold rush near Iditarod began, 1908, sled dog racing fever had gripped residents of Nome, by that time a prosperous city, and the Nome Kennel Club was organized. The club sponsored several races of different lengths, one of which took advantage of a segment of the Iditarod Trail. The 65-mile Solomon Derby, held in February or March, went from Nome to Solomon and back, and was considered a warm-up for the longer All Alaska Sweepstakes.

Dog racing also took hold in other towns. On New Year's Day, 1911, the first annual Iditarod Sweepstakes ran from Iditarod to Flat, with a grand prize of $350. Residents of Iditarod formed a kennel club and sponsored men's and women's sled dog races. The Ruby Dog Derby, a 58-mile race held from Ruby, on the Yukon River, south to Long City and back, traced a section of the even-year route of the modern Iditarod Trail Sled Dog Race. The Anchorage Kennel Club's first race, in 1916, followed a section of the Iditarod Trail from Anchorage to Old Knik and back. A hand-printed sign from that event reveals conditions hundreds of mushers have faced since then: "weather bad, 10 below...heavy north wind."

Dog racing wasn't the only excitement in town. On February 21, 1924, Ben Eielson flew the first official mail plane between Fairbanks and McGrath, 275 miles in about three hours. He'd pushed for several years to get a mail route, and finally succeeded; the U.S. Postal Service paid him two dollars per mile, about half the cost of mail delivery between these two towns by dog team, which took 12 days. Throughout the next few years, aviation technology continued to improve, airmail routes replacing dog team deliveries. Anchorage, too, was growing, drawing workers from Interior goldfields to the fledgling city. No longer did hundreds tramp the Iditarod Trail. By the end of the 1920s, much of it had disappeared, alders and willows claiming its edges, muskegs swallowing its trace. ■

By Susan Beeman, Associate Editor

This was the land of the midnight sun and it held romance, that kind of romance that does not require the presence of a woman, although a woman would have improved the situation.
— Charles Lee Cadwallader, circa 1917,
*Reminiscences of the Iditarod Trail:
Placer Mining Days in Alaska,*
date of publication unknown

Roadhouse Tales

Charles Lee Cadwallader's musing reflects the spirit of those traveling the Iditarod Trail during the early 1900s: men under the spell of wilderness. But wilderness sufficed for only so long, and even tough miners and mushers (walkers and dog team drivers) needed a home-cooked meal and a bed every now and then. Roadhouses provided these services.

The term "roadhouse" is relative. Those along the Iditarod Trail ranged from musty tents in camps slapped hastily together beside the trail to luxury two-story structures in fledgling towns. A roadhouse was often the first business to open in a new mining area; the rest of the town soon followed. Some arose casually. Travelers, mostly miners and mail carriers, would show up at a cabin or house and spend the night, and the owner, pleased with the profit, would begin catering to guests on a regular basis. Beds were sometimes only simple bunks with no mattresses or with spruce boughs for cushioning. Roadhouses allowed mail carriers certain privileges; many let the drivers' lead dog sleep inside and offered a barn or stable for housing the rest of the team overnight. Drivers ate breakfast before other guests and their wet clothes were hung nearest the fire.

Some miners kept accounts of traversing the trail, including details about clothing, people, and lodging. Cadwallader set out from Anchorage on his way to Iditarod in April 1917, and by the time the office worker-turned-prospector reached Mrs. Johnson's and Billy Dennison's Little Susitna Roadhouse, 14 miles west of Knik, his feet and legs ached, so after eating, he bathed his feet in a basin. The transition from desk clerk to mountain man did not go smoothly, but it was, by necessity, rapid. Cadwallader stumbled into Mountain Climber's Roadhouse, about halfway between Old Skwentna and Finger Lake, ready to collapse from fatigue and sore muscles. "The custom of the Roadhouse keepers," he writes, "is to serve tea and a dish of fruit upon the arrival of the musher," and then allow the traveler a rest before serving a meal. "A tired musher is not hungry." But according to Skwentna resident Joe Delia, who's lived in the area

The Cape Nome Roadhouse, 14 miles east of Nome, was built about 1900 during the rush to dig gold from the Bering Sea town's beaches and creeks. Today, Nome's hotels and houses fill quickly during race time as fans gather to welcome mushers across the finish line. (Hegg 1637, Special Collections Division, University of Washington Libraries)

since 1949 and has collected a wealth of stories from others, the roadhouse's owner, nicknamed Mountain Climber, "was an old grouch who fed poorly and put up travelers in a cold tent." Whatever the truth, Cadwallader wasn't cowed, for this is where he penned his thoughts on the journey's romance.

Alice McDonald, or "Mrs. Mac" as she became known, moved in 1910 to the community of Iditarod, where she founded the McDonald Hotel, one of the leading establishments during the town's heyday. A 1984 *Alaska Journal* article makes clear the lodge owner's role during the gold rush; says McDonald, "People would come in at all hours of the night for their rooms or their bunks. But they treated me with the greatest of respect and I had all kinds of different nationalities of people staying there. Many times when a man came in from the creeks he would throw me his gold poke and say, 'Keep it until I leave.' I would carefully put it under my bunk. The honesty among miners you would never find in any other place." McDonald herself had immigrated to America from Sweden and lived briefly in Canada with her husband, an unsuccessful miner.

Kenneth Gideon describes the Takotna Roadhouse as a "primitive [log] affair" chinked with anything. Of its proprietors, he says Mrs. McLean "was Scotch Presbyterian, a short chunk of a woman. In her natural stance her head was thrust forward and her eyes were slightly screwed up as if she were peering through a fog. It was when she leaned back and stared at you over one shoulder with her eyes wide that you felt it necessary to seek cover." Mrs. McLean had owned a placer mine, but it never made her rich; before that she'd traded furs. Gideon also recounted the operator's relationship with her husband, a former boat captain nicknamed "Sandbar McLean"

In the early 1900s, Knik, with its roadhouses and stores, was a major supply stop for miners heading to the Iditarod area. "Knik," a Dena'ina Indian name meaning "fire," originally referred to several settlements at the head of Cook Inlet. Today, Knik is often called the "dog mushing center of the world." Many Iditarod mushers call the area home, including the Redingtons. (B81.19.18, Anchorage Museum of History and Art)

One of several roadhouses for mail carriers, the original building at Rohn burned down long ago. Today's cabin was built in the 1930s and is managed by the Bureau of Land Management. Josiah E. Spurr named the location after Oscar Rohn, member of an 1898 USGS expedition that traveled through the Alaska Range and down the Kuskokwim River. Rohn marks the transition from mountains to the flat land of the Interior. (Harry M. Walker)

for his frequent aquatic groundings. "When she spoke to him, it was in much the same tone of voice that she might have used on a well-trained Newfoundland dog, which he somewhat resembled, having a large head, bushy hair, a walrus moustache, and a chunky body with short legs which carried him down the road with a waddle." Gideon's many tales of the Iditarod Trail reside in his 1967 book *Wandering Boy: Alaska — 1913 to 1918*.

Cadwallader, having toughened, returned to Anchorage from Iditarod in December 1918 and recalls setting out alone on foot from Rohn Road-

house into an impending blizzard. "Richards, the Roadhouse man, made for me a sourdough lantern by taking a size 2-1/2 tomato can, punched a hole in the side of the can for an ordinary tallow candle, then tied a dish cloth over the open end of the can so the wind would not blow a light out." Later, nearly 50 miles farther south, he arrived at Claus Anderson's Rainy Pass Roadhouse only to find it deserted and devoid of food, so he built a fire, ate a few bites from the bread loaf in his pocket, then curled up "on a black bear skin and went to sleep." He eventually made it back to Knik. □

The 1925 Serum Run

By Penny Rennick, Editor

EDITOR'S NOTE: *The relay of medicine to Nome by sled dog teams that has come to be known as the Serum Run gained worldwide attention 76 years ago. There were actually two relays; this article addresses the first. Reports differ on the exact order of the mushers on the Interior portion of the relays and newspaper accounts from the time are inconclusive. In recent years the Serum Run has been commemorated with a sled dog caravan from Nenana to Nome concurrent with the Iditarod race.*

Leonhard Seppala and lead dog Togo pose at Nome. A natural leader, Togo came from the line of dogs chosen to haul explorer Roald Amundsen to the North Pole. As a young dog, Togo couldn't be contained. One day when Seppala set out on a long-distance run, he left instructions for his handler to keep the dog in an enclosure. Instead, Togo tried to climb the fence. He reached the top but got hung up on the far side by his foot. He yelped and the handler came to help him. While doing so, Togo twisted free and ran off, following Seppala and his team who already had several hours head-start. The musher later reported that when he looked up the towline as his dogs were moving, he saw a dog running loose at the head of his team, nipping at the ear of his lead dogs. From then on, Togo became Seppala's number one leader. (Courtesy of the Carrie McLain Museum)

In late January 1925 diphtheria struck the frontier town of Nome, barricaded behind the ice of the Bering Sea on western Alaska's Seward Peninsula. The only reliable way of reaching Nome in winter was by dog team. When the epidemic struck, Dr. Curtis Welch, a Public Health Service (PHS) physician and the only doctor in town, checked his limited supply of antitoxin and found it more than a year old. His request the previous summer for a fresh supply had gone unfulfilled and more antitoxin was mandatory to prevent a full-blown epidemic from ravaging the community.

Dr. Welch sent an immediate plea for antitoxin to the PHS's Seattle regional office. Geography would prevent that supply from reaching Nome before the diphtheria infected others. A second message was telegraphed to Fairbanks, Seward, Anchorage, and Juneau. Moving quickly, Nome city officials quarantined the town to keep the highly contagious disease from spreading. They established a Board of Health, headed by M. L. Summers of Hammon Consolidated Gold Fields, to enforce the quarantine and to mobilize the community against the disease. The board discussed options to expeditiously get the antitoxin to Nome, should anyone in Alaska have a supply they could send. A flight from Fairbanks was proposed but rejected because aviation was still in its infancy in Alaska and a wintertime flight was deemed too risky. Finally the board settled on a dog team run from

Nenana, the closest rail stop, as the best solution. Now they had to find the nearest antitoxin.

Dr. J.B. Beeson of the Alaska Railroad Hospital in Anchorage had a fresh supply of 300,000 units; 30,000 units was the preferred dose for those who already had the disease, but a much smaller amount could immunize those who had been exposed but had not contracted diphtheria. Territorial governor Scott Bone agreed that the railroad and dog teams were the best transportation to get the Anchorage serum to Nome and the governor's staff arranged for Northern Commercial Company (NCC) to provide dog teams along the route from Nenana to Nome.

In the early twentieth century, NCC was the largest commercial enterprise in Alaska's Interior. It operated trading posts and river steamers and also had the contract to deliver mail from Fairbanks along the Tanana and Yukon River valleys to Unalakleet. From November to May, contracted mushers and dog teams delivered mail and supplies throughout much of the Interior. The governor's staff telegraphed E.G. Wetzler, Railway Mail Service chief clerk in Nenana, instructing him to send the following message to U.S. Signal Corps stations between Nenana and the Bering coast: "Request the best musher and team in your section to stand by to receive the serum for Nome starting from Nenana tomorrow."

Regular mail drivers were alerted, and Signal Corpsmen visited nearby Native villages, seeking the most skilled mushers and fastest dogs. These efforts produced 15 dog teams, usually an amalgam of the swiftest dogs in a settlement. As Kenneth A. Ungermann wrote in *The Race To Nome* (1963), "Often a team was formed from the individually fastest dogs in a village and loaned to the man who was acknowledged to be the best musher. Warmest fur clothes were donned, harness and sleds were checked.... [Then] the chosen teams drifted out of the birch and alder thickets and the silent spruce stands to the mail shelter cabins along the 450-mile trail to Unalakleet."

1925 Serum Run

127 1/2 hours, 674 miles*

Jan. 27-28:	Wild Bill Shannon, Nenana to Tolovana (52 miles)
28:	Dan Green, Tolovana to Manley Hot Springs (31 miles)
28:	Johnny Folger, Manley Hot Springs to Fish Lake (28 miles)
29:	Sam Joseph, Fish Lake to Tanana (26 miles)
29:	Titus Nikoli, Tanana to Kallands (34 miles)
29:	Dave Corning, Kallands to Nine Mile mail cabin (24 miles)
29:	Edgar Kalland, Nine Mile cabin to Kokrines (30 miles)
29:	Harry Pitka, Kokrines to Ruby (30 miles)
29:	Bill McCarty, Ruby to Whiskey Creek (28 miles)
29-30:	Edgar Nollner, Whiskey Creek to Galena (24 miles)
30:	George Nollner, Galena to Bishop Mountain (18 miles)
30:	Charlie Evans, Bishop Mountain to Nulato (30 miles)
30:	Tommy Patsy, Nulato to Kaltag (36 miles)
30:	Jackscrew, Kaltag to Old Woman shelter house (40 miles)
30-31:	Victor Anagick, Old Woman to Unalakleet (34 miles)
31:	Myles Gonangnan, Unalakleet to Shaktoolik (40 miles)
31:	Henry Ivanoff, Leaves from Shaktoolik toward Golovin but meets Leonhard Seppala who returns to Golovin
31:	Leonhard Seppala, Shaktoolik to Golovin (91 miles)
Feb. 1:	Charlie Olson, Golovin to Bluff (25 miles)
1-2:	Gunnar Kaasen, Bluff to Nome (53 miles)

* Mileage from Kenneth A. Ungermann's interviews with serum mushers and his account of the event, *The Race To Nome* (1963).

Back in Anchorage, Dr. Beeson bundled the vials containing the serum in a cylinder protected with quilting and wrapped in canvas, total weight, 20 pounds. Monday, January 26, he handed the package to Frank Knight, Alaska Railroad conductor, who would oversee the serum's 298-mile journey by rail to Nenana. The antitoxin was on its way to Nome.

In Nome, the Board of Health had chosen champion musher Leonhard Seppala to travel by dog team to the Yukon Valley, perhaps as far upriver as Nulato, to meet the team or teams coming downriver from

Rick Swenson and Vern Halter arrive at Shaktoolik, an Inupiaq community of 230 on the shore of Norton Sound. During the 1925 Serum Run, Henry Ivanoff was just north of town when he spotted the Siberian huskies of Leonhard Seppala coming toward him out of the blowing snow. Seppala almost drove past Ivanoff in his rush to reach the Yukon Valley, not realizing that the serum had been relayed from the Interior to the coast. (Jeff Schultz/Alaska Stock)

Nenana with the serum. Seppala worked for Hammon Consolidated Gold Fields, headed by Summers. The company paid to feed Seppala's dogs; in return, the animals were used as company sled dogs. Seppala planned to take two teams, beginning with 20 dogs and dropping 12 along the way. On his return, he would replace tired or injured dogs with the animals that had been dropped. Leading his teams was a light-gray, 48-pound, Siberian husky named Togo.

Tuesday, January 27. The train reached Nenana about 11 P.M., where Knight handed the package to Wild Bill Shannon, who with nine malamutes undertook the first leg of the relay to Nome. A regular mail driver, Shannon had remained in the Tanana Valley region after his discharge from the Army's Quartermaster Corps. He guided his team along the Tanana Valley 52 miles to Tolovana where, by most accounts, he passed the serum to his friend Dan Green, who headed for Manley Hot Springs. [Other sources list Edgar Kalland or "Tolovana Jim" Kalland as the next musher.] From Manley to Fish Lake to Tanana, near that river's junction with the mighty Yukon, the serum sped westward. Johnny Folger and Sam Joseph, both Athabaskan Indians, mushed their malamutes over a trail they knew well. In temperatures of nearly 40 below, Joseph reached Tanana on Thursday, January 29, traveling 26 miles at an average speed of more than nine miles per hour.

Meanwhile, the previous day Seppala had left Nome on his way east to meet the relay. M.L. Summers's instructions to the Norwegian were to travel slowly at first, saving his team for the long return to Nome. What the miner did not tell the musher was that the serum was being relayed and that it was already farther along the route to Nome than anyone expected.

Back in the Interior, Titus Nickoli carried the 20-pound package on the stretch from Tanana to Kallands, a roadhouse on the north shore of the Yukon. On and on the serum went, past Birches, past Kokrines where Harry Pitka picked it up and sprinted for Ruby. The previous year Pitka had been hired to deliver the mail, but his contract was not renewed for the winter of 1924-25. He hoped to resume mail delivery the following winter. At Ruby, Bill McCarty waited with seven dogs from Alex Brown's team, led by Prince. Ruby had gained fame for its Ruby Derby, a sled dog race, and Brown's teams were frequent winners. With temperatures hovering at minus 40 at Whiskey Creek, headquarters for mail teams along this section of the Yukon Valley, McCarty turned the serum over to 18-year-old Edgar Nollner and his leader, Dixie, who would carry on to Galena. George Nollner, Edgar's older brother, waited there to push on to Bishop Mountain.

The next relay musher, Charlie Evans, piloted boats through the shifting channels of the Yukon River in summer. But five o'clock this Friday morning, January 30th, 54 hours out from Nenana, Evans and his team were headed into cold, with lows reported at 64 below. At those temperatures open water can create deadly hazards where a trail crosses

FAR LEFT: *Serum musher Edgar Kalland of Kaltag died in 1983. (Bill Devine)*

LEFT: *Charlie Evans mushed the diphtheria serum from Bishop Mountain to Nulato. Charlie wears a hat of marten fur that he made. He gave a similar hat to Anchorage resident and Iditarod supporter Bill Devine in thanks for Devine's help on a visit to Anchorage. (Bill Devine)*

major rivers. Evans encountered just such circumstances where the east fork of the Koyukuk River, a major tributary, enters the Yukon. Evans was forced to detour around the open water, cutting through patches of dense ice fog where only his dogs' head and tail were visible. The groins of two dogs borrowed to complete the team began to freeze in the extreme cold. The musher had to keep the team moving; there was nothing he could do for the freezing dogs, who later died.

At Nulato, Evans's ordeal ended. Now it was Tommy Patsy's turn to carry the serum. Cold temperatures, daylight, and a hard-packed trail sped the Athabaskan on his way, 36 miles in three and one-half hours, more than 10 miles per hour, the fastest individual speed of any of the serum mushers. At Kaltag the trail headed inland, across the Kaltag Portage, past Old Woman to the Bering Sea Inupiaq community of Unalakleet. The portage is well

As a child, Edith Iyatunguk, in fur hat with blanket, received some of the serum that the relay teams carried from Nenana to Nome. With Edith in Nome are (from left) Col. Norman Vaughn, Iditarod musher and a leader of the Serum Run commemoration, Iditarod musher Herbie Nayokpuk, and an unidentified woman. (William Foster)

known to today's Iditarod mushers, just as it was to the mail drivers of the past.

While Jackscrew, another Athabaskan, and his team climbed through the Nulato Hills toward the coast and Leonhard Seppala and Togo hurried along the coast of Norton Sound toward the Yukon Valley, diphtheria cases piled up in Nome. The growing emergency prompted the Board of Health to send two more mushers with fresh teams along the route to await Seppala's return. Gunnar Kaasen, using dogs that Seppala had left behind and with Balto in the lead, headed to Bluff with a message for Charlie Olson, owner of the roadhouse at Bluff, to head east to Golovin to meet Seppala. Kaasen was to wait at Bluff to take the serum from Olson and hurry to Nome. Later another well-known local musher, Ed Rohn, and his fast sprint team, were sent to Safety, 22 miles east of Nome, to wait for Kaasen. Summers and the Board of Health took one final step to speed the serum's travels. They telegraphed Charles Traeger, storekeeper at Unalakleet, to spend whatever it took to have fresh teams standing by to carry the serum until they could meet up with Seppala.

By 9:10 P.M. Friday, Jackscrew and the serum had arrived at Old Woman cabin, 34 miles from Unalakleet. Now an Eskimo, Victor Anagick, loaded the parcel into his sled for the downhill run to the coast. Anagick clerked for Traeger and was driving the storekeeper's team. He had gone to Old Woman when Summers's message had reached Traeger to provide more teams. By 3:30 Saturday morning the serum had reached the Bering Sea, 465 miles from Nenana and another 207 trail miles from Nome.

With a storm building and without the protection of the forested river valleys of the Interior, 28-year-old musher Myles Gonangnan, a full-blooded Eskimo and lifelong resident of Unalakleet, followed instructions from Traeger's assistant Ed Bradley, to travel along the coast rather than cut across the ice of Norton Sound. New snow would slow his team and he was told to stop at Eban, an Eskimo settlement 25 miles out, to warm the serum. He was then to continue to Shaktoolik, where Henry Ivanoff waited for the serum. Gonangnan transferred the package to Ivanoff and the half Russian, half Eskimo headed out.

A half mile north of Shaktoolik Ivanoff had stopped to disentangle his team when he noticed a dog team of Siberian huskies racing his way. Most people in this part of Alaska knew of Leonhard Seppala and his famous huskies, the only team of this breed in the Serum Run. The Norwegian almost drove past Ivanoff without stopping because Ivanoff's words that he had the serum were being carried off by the wind and because Seppala didn't expect to receive the serum until he reached Nulato. He didn't know about the relay that had carried the package down the Yukon and across the portage to the coast.

Once the serum was safely stowed in Seppala's sled and the musher had the instructions for its care, he turned back north into the wind with temperatures at minus 30 and the storm howling.

Seppala was headed to Golovin, 91 miles away; the shortest route was straight across 20 miles of sea ice to Isaac's Point. Seppala's experience, Togo's leadership, and the team's trail savvy lead the musher to risk crossing the open ice rather than traveling the much longer distance along the shore. The Norwegian maintained that among Togo's greatest assets in open terrain was his penchant for the direct approach, the shortest distance between two points. Seppala indicated where he wanted to go. Togo drew a bead on the goal and off the team went, with Togo never deviating from the straight line. Seppala and the serum set out across open sea ice, trusting Togo to get them safely to the opposite shore. At 8 P.M. Saturday they made it, 84 miles in one day, averaging more than seven miles per hour and facing a strong headwind for half the distance. After feeding and resting the dogs for the night at a cabin near Isaac's Point, Seppala resumed the race Sunday morning, with the blizzard still howling. However, he followed the last-minute advice of an Eskimo

elder who watched him pack his sled. Instead of traveling far out on the ice on the route to Golovin, Seppala stayed closer to shore. A wise decision, since the wind had pushed the ice over which he traveled the previous day out to sea.

Finally Seppala reached Golovin where Charlie Olson undertook the next leg of the relay, the storm still raging. A bachelor at age 46, Olson had lived his entire adult life in the Alaska Bush. At 3:15 P.M. Sunday he headed into the storm, on his way to Bluff. With his seven malamutes lead by Jack, Olson left Golovin in 30 below, with the wind blowing 40 miles per hour. His 25-mile leg turned out to be the toughest of the relay. Ungermann reports: "As Olson came to Golovin Lagoon, a storm gust funneling though a valley in the low hills to his right struck him with hurricane force. The sled, the dogs, and Olson were lifted bodily and were hurled from the trail." Olson and the dogs were blown off the trail

Edgar Nollner, one of the original serum mushers, is flanked by Joe Redington (left) and Anchorage artist and photographer Bill Devine in this photo taken on Nome's Front Street. (Courtesy of Bill Devine)

more than once, but they struggled on. At 7:30 that evening he arrived at Bluff, only 53 miles from Nome. Olson's dogs were severely frozen when they reached Bluff Sunday evening and several later died.

Now it was Gunnar Kaasen's turn. Controversy surrounds Kaasen's role in the Serum Run, but there is no denying that the musher, another Norwegian, and his leader, Balto, actually one of Seppala's freight dogs, got the serum to Nome. Although not a well-known musher, Kaasen worked for the same company as Seppala. He was strong and steady, and he chose a long-haired, big freight dog with a white front right leg to lead his team. Kaasen was supposed to take the serum as far as Safety and hand it over to Ed Rohn and his speedy team for the run into Nome.

Darkness and blowing snow that forced the dogs to plow through drifts up to their belly and Kaasen to break trail in drifts reaching to his chest slowed their pace. Finally the musher and team circled the snow ridge blocking the path and the dogs surged forward onto a firm trail. Later, as they were crossing the Topkok River, Balto stopped abruptly. Kaasen urged the dog forward but he refused to move. When Kaasen walked up to him at the front of the team, he found the dog standing in overflow, where river water had reached the surface through a crack in the ice. Balto had averted disaster. Quickly Kaasen unhitched the leader and led him to fresh snow where the dog could dry his feet.

Although Summers had telephoned Solomon Roadhouse with instructions for the serum mushers to wait out the storm in Solomon, Kaasen passed just to the south of town and didn't see the roadhouse. Not until two miles farther along the trail did he spot familiar landmarks that told him his next stop would be Safety. But the wind wasn't through with him yet. A gust flipped the sled and some of the dogs. With the team and sled straightened, Kaasen felt for the serum package. Gone. Frantically the musher searched the snow in darkness until his hand touched the bundle. Kaasen retied it to his sled and with the wind now at his back, raced for Safety.

When he arrived, Ed Rohn was asleep because he had received the message from Nome telling Kaasen to wait at Solomon. Kaasen continued to Nome rather than waking Rohn, a decision that stirred controversy for years. At 5:30 Monday morning, five and one-third days after the serum left Nenana, Balto led Gunnar Kaasen onto Front Street in Nome. Balto and the other dogs had covered 53 miles in seven and one-half hours.

Balto and Togo remain the two most renowned leaders of the Serum Run. Balto is on display in Cleveland where he lived out his years at the zoo after being purchased by a businessman who saw the dog in a traveling side show in California and thought he deserved better for his deeds in the Serum Run. The businessman organized a penny drive among Cleveland's children to help fund Balto's quarters at the zoo. Togo stands front and center at Iditarod Headquarters in Wasilla, Alaska, the first thing visitors see when they come through the door. □

In the 1970s, the surviving serum mushers gathered in Anchorage. Front row center is Bill McCarty; back row center are Charlie Evans, Edgar Kalland, and Edgar Nollner. Harry Pitka was also alive at the time the photo was taken, but he was under nursing care at an Anchorage facility. Pitka died in 1979. Artist Bill Devine kneels front row right; the other individuals are unidentified. (Courtesy of Bill Devine)

Redington and Page: "Parents" of the Iditarod

By Susan Beeman

EDITOR'S NOTE: *Joe Redington Sr. and Dorothy G. Page are often referred to as the "Father" and "Mother" of the Iditarod, their contributions to the success of the race legendary. Each had a passion for dog mushing and the Iditarod Trail.*

When Wasilla reporter Kathleen Tessaro asked Joe Redington in a 1998 interview if mushing in cold weather was hard on an older man, he replied, "Hell yes. The only thing I can think of that age don't hurt is a diamond. I'll tell you one thing though, I'd like to have run the Iditarod when I was 35." Redington, shown here with his famous lead dog Feets, entered the Iditarod for the first time in 1974. He was 56. (Bill Devine)

I don't have to win to have fun.
— Joe Redington Sr., 1917-1999

Midwest, 1920s, a boy skipping recess to read books: as a poor child being raised by his father, Joe Redington read every story about Alaska and the north he could get his hands on — the All-Alaska Sweepstakes, the 1925 diphtheria serum run, Leonhard Seppala's mushing adventures. Redington knew he wanted a dog team.

After a stint in the Army during World War II and several less-than-challenging jobs, Redington made a snap decision to head to Alaska. Fueled by a troubled marriage and his long-held dream of pursuing a wilderness existence, Redington traveled the newly built Alaska-Canada Highway in 1948, accompanied by his son Joee; his brother, Ray, and Ray's family; and seven mixed-breed dogs. Redington's wife, Cathy, stayed behind to have their second child, Raymie; they would join Redington in Alaska later. Vi (Hoffman) Redington, then Ray's wife, later divorced him and married Joe, who had by then divorced his first wife.

It didn't take long for Joe and Vi to fall in love with Alaska and establish a homestead in Knik. They opened Knik Kennels in 1949 along what then was only a muddy track, now Knik-Goose Bay Road. Today's Iditarod race route passes the kennel before heading west toward the Susitna River.

Early in his introduction to Alaska, Redington met Knik neighbor Lee Ellexson, a former Iditarod Trail mail carrier and operator of the Happy River Roadhouse, 14 miles northwest of Puntilla Lake in Rainy Pass. Ellexson's stories of handmade dog sleds and dangerous creek-crossings enchanted Redington, who thrived on hunting, fishing, and training his team.

In the 1950s, Redington was back in service to the United States military, not as an enlisted man but as a civilian whose talents and equipment they sought. With his dog team, the musher could access remote plane crash sites that motorized vehicles could not, assisting in salvage operations. Big-game guiding also provided income.

Drawn to Anchorage each year during the Fur Rendezvous winter carnival, the Redingtons began entering sprint races in the mid 1950s. Joe's first attempt at the World Championship Sled Dog Race, then dominated by Gareth Wright, George Attla (known as the "Huslia Hustler" for his speed), and Roland Lombard, was dismal — he scratched. His sons, Joee and Raymie, however, ascended the ranks of successful racers in the late 1950s and early 1960s while Redington continued his low-key style of mushing for fun and hauling freight. He liked being out on the old Iditarod Trail near his homestead with just his dogs for company, without the pressure of speed racing.

When we started opening the trail out of Knik, people said it was impossible…that was the wrong thing to tell me!
— Dorothy G. Page, 1921-1989

Dorothy G. Page was born in Michigan and raised in Minneapolis. In 1960 she moved to Alaska with her husband, Von. The couple had planned only to visit but ended up staying, making their home first in Dillingham, then Wasilla. Page had previously owned a café and a trading post in New Mexico; she thrived on challenges.

Page's interest in her new community's history prompted her to form the Wasilla-Knik-Willow Creek Historical Society. She also chaired the town's Alaska Centennial Committee, organized to commemorate the Alaska Purchase of 1867. As a historian, Page knew how important the pioneers, most of whom traveled by dog team, had been to Alaska's early years, forming a network of trails and communications throughout the territory. The rising use of snow machines and fading public interest in dog mushing plagued her vision of what Alaska should be, and Page began to wonder what effect a dog race

Like so many before and after, Dorothy Page came to Alaska planning only to stay a short time, but Alaska's spell captured her and her husband, and they became residents. As a historian and community activist, Page helped rekindle the spirit of dog mushing at a time when airplanes and snow machines threatened to take over canine power. Even before the Iditarod became world-famous, Page reported on each year's race in the Iditarod Trail Annual. *(Jeff Schultz/ Alaska Stock)*

to celebrate the centennial might have. Von owned a team, but as superintendent of Wasilla's schools, he had little time to run or train them, let alone help organize a race. Others Page approached resisted her "weird idea," pronouncing it "too much work."

Then Page met Redington at Willow's Winter Carnival. He immediately embraced her idea. Both members of Aurora Dog Mushers, a local club, they hoped to see mushing make a comeback and the Iditarod Trail resurrected. The club appointed an "Iditarod Trail Committee," setting the wheels in motion. Despite the unknowns — trail condition, origin of prize money, and even who would enter the race — the committee forged ahead with plans for the 56-mile Centennial Purchase race of 1967, the precursor to today's Iditarod Trail Sled Dog Race. □

From Anchorage to Nome:
The Evolving Race

The Early Years

With a $25,000 purse attached to the Centennial Iditarod, interest in winning this new race was high. But there was a catch, at least for Joe Redington. Though he'd promised this figure on behalf of the Iditarod Trail Committee, he had no idea how they would raise the money.

Then he got an idea. He and Vi sold one-square-foot parcels from what they dubbed "The Centennial Acre" on their second homestead on Flat Horn Lake, west of Knik. They made $12,000. The chief of the Tyonek Athabaskan tribe from northwestern Cook Inlet offered another $15,000, but only as a loan, and only if Redington had collateral. He did — his homestead.

Fund-raising took time away from trail clearing. Only nine miles of the historic Iditarod Trail near Knik were reopened, forcing the race route to veer north onto an existing trail toward Big Lake, 28 miles away. By race day, sandwiched on the calendar in February between Anchorage's World Championship and Fairbanks's North American Championship Sled Dog Races, 59 mushers massed at the starting line for the round-trip adventure. An array of people entered, among them Inupiaq musher Herbie Nayokpuk, Redington and his sons Joee and Raymie, World Championship Sled Dog Race winners Gareth Wright and Roland Lombard, and future Iditarod champions Dick Mackey and Jerry Riley. Isaac Okleasik of Teller, on the Seward Peninsula, won. Most other teams completed the race, considered in 1967 to be long distance.

Hobbled by sick dogs and lack of time spent training, Redington barely made it to the finish line. Bad weather the next year forced the race's cancellation, and in 1969 it made a weak return with only 12 mushers signed up and $1,000 offered to the winners. The snow machine, or "iron dog," had arrived in Alaska, faster and easier to maintain than real dogs. "People didn't have to feed the snow machines," Redington later wrote.

Disappointment at this new trend and the low turnout for the second Iditarod race shed light on what it would take to put the Iditarod Trail back on the map and recapture dog mushing before it was gone forever. Maybe, Redington figured, if they staged a long, round-trip race between Knik and the ghost town of Iditarod, it would generate new enthusiasm. One thousand miles wasn't too much to ask, was it? He had to try.

But apathy and resistance met him at each turn. People had never heard of the old town of Iditarod, or they balked at the length of the proposed route. Redington, ever the optimist, considered an idea Dorothy Page had proposed when she'd initially approached him about the Centennial race — reestablish the Iditarod Trail all the way to Nome.

FACING PAGE: *Iditarod veterinarian Carol Griffitts examines a dog at Nikolai, about one-third of the way through the race. In the 1990s, a few sponsors pulled out of the Iditarod under pressure from animal rights groups, but others stepped in to replace them. (Jeff Schultz/Alaska Stock)*

Preposterous! people said. *What is that man thinking?* To the alarm of the ITC, Redington also proposed that a guaranteed $50,000 purse accompany the race. The Aurora Dog Mushers club, to which all the ITC members belonged, abandoned the committee along with their support of Redington's ambitious venture. No one wanted to be responsible for the prize money. With only three advocates left standing at his side — teachers Tom Johnson and Gleo Huyck, and his wife, Vi — Redington

incorporated the ITC, the four of them its officers. Publicity about the proposed race to Nome only widened the base of naysayers; then, quietly at first, a few advocates emerged, among them Alaska Native elders, experts on working dogs who knew the teams could mush that far. Redington spent the next couple of years raising money and working out the details.

Mushers George Attla of Huslia, Ken Chase of Anvik, and Dick Mackey of Wasilla heard about the race and signed

on for the challenge. Others declared their intentions to race. Redington wrote to an acquaintance, Howard Farley, in Nome, asking for help in clearing the north end of the trail and promoting what the ITC was calling the "Iditarod Trail International Championship Race." (That letter is on display today at Rasmussen's Music Mart in Nome.) More mushers signed up. Days before the scheduled start, the ITC still sought allies and funding.

Three key people jumped in to help. Col. Marvin "Muktuk" Marston, organizer of the Alaska Territorial Guard during World War II and Redington's longtime friend, pledged $10,000. Having traveled extensively around the Arctic by dogsled, himself a pioneer, Marston was sympathetic to Redington's cause. Senator Frank Murkowski, then president of Bank of the North, authorized a sizeable loan. Businessman and politician Bruce Kendall, who predicted the race would help promote tourism while supporting the spirit of Alaska, co-signed with Redington on the loan for $30,000. Another $10,000 trickled in from individual donations. All the funds weren't in the ITC's bank account when the mushers left the Anchorage chute for Nome on March 3, 1973, but by the time

A musher travels through the Farewell Burn, about 40 miles across and littered with dead, charred trees from a 1979 forest fire. The expanse is notoriously windy, and mushers often express relief at putting it behind them. (Jeff Schultz/Alaska Stock)

1989 race winner Joe Runyan steers a traditional wooden sled through the crowd. Though longer and slower than modern sleds, the baskets of these old workhorses hold more freight than today's racing toboggans. The first man to triumph again after four consecutive years of victorious women, Runyan lifted his fellow male competitors' spirits in an ongoing friendly rivalry between men and women for the Iditarod championship. (Barb Willard)

the first musher, Dick Wilmarth, crossed the finish line 20 days, 49 minutes, 41 seconds later, the purse was legitimate and the ITC, with relief, awarded the winners their promised prize money.

Let the Long Race Begin!

The 1978 Iditarod champion, Dick Mackey, likened the inaugural race to a "big camping trip." It's doubtful many veteran mushers would call it that today, considering the financial stakes involved. The increase in cost of running the race and in the purse itself are two of many changes throughout the years; equipment is different now, mushing experience is mandatory, and ethical dilemmas concerning dog care are being addressed. One thing, though, has remained constant: Training for and running the race requires a huge commitment of time, money, and hard work.

Early attitudes about the long race ranged from skeptical to confident. One thousand miles by dog sled from Anchorage to Nome — most people thought Redington's idea was crazy. Who would clear the trail? Redington didn't

know. Where would they get the cash to pay the winning mushers? Redington didn't know. Could people even mush that far? Of course, Redington told them, people had mushed long distance before, why not now?

Still, even some of the mushers who ran the first race remained skeptical until they neared Nome. Attla, in his book *The Iditarod: the Most Demanding Race of All* (1974), says, "...this Iditarod race is not a race at all.... You are just traveling. If you

pushed your dogs they couldn't make 1,000 miles." Attla, however, even with a permanently locked knee from surgery after childhood tuberculosis, finished the race in fourth place and won $4,000, just one of 22 men who proved it possible.

Others shaped views of the race in its infancy, too. In 1974, Lolly Medley and Mary Shields were the first women to run. Shields, who beat Medley across the finish line by just 29 minutes to place 23rd, recalls someone at the starting line

ABOVE: *Alaska Native mushers like Victor Kotongan from Unalakleet used sturdy village dogs the first few years of the Iditarod. In 1973, he placed 15th, finishing in just less than 29 days; his winnings that year totaled $800. (Bill Devine)*

ABOVE, RIGHT: *Ken Chase of Anvik, the southernmost checkpoint on the Yukon River during odd-numbered years, fed his dogs "bear meat, green frozen fish, and commercial feed," according to the 1975* Iditarod Trail Annual. *Anvik's residents "gave the mushers a tremendous reception." Chase entered the Iditarod 15 times. (Marydith Beeman)*

hollering, "You better turn around now, you'll never make it." Eighteen years later, Shields and several other mushers created the educational organization

Mush with P.R.I.D.E. (Providing Responsible Education on a Dog's Environment), dedicated to the care and treatment of sled dogs and helping the public learn more about mushing. Shields never ran the Iditarod again. Medley entered her second race in 1984, but broke her kneecap, flew to Anchorage to have a thigh-to-ankle cast put on, continued racing for five more days, then had to scratch. Exhibiting a different kind of perseverance, Terry Adkins, the only veterinarian on the trail during the 1973 race, entered the Iditarod 21 times between 1974 and 1998, mustering his first team from the Anchorage animal shelter. All 12 of the dogs with which he began the race pulled him across the finish line. Adkins made it into the top 10 three times, scratched three times, and finished the other races in modest form; his years of competition embody the experience of many Iditarod mushers — consistently running with the middle of the pack, a position short on glory, yet

long on adventure, and at the least offering a sense of accomplishment. Race pioneers like Medley, Shields, Adkins, and others set the stage for a race in which a wide variety of people and goals are welcome.

Volunteer support for the Iditarod continued to grow throughout the 1970s. Friends and acquaintances heard of the race and offered their services. Bill Devine was one such enthusiast. Listening to the first Iditarod on the radio had piqued his interest, and soon after, he met Redington. "By god," Devine told him, "you're gonna need some help." Devine, retired from the U.S. Air Force and an artist and photographer in Anchorage, began shooting the race and promoting it each year. He designed the ITC logo, set up race headquarters at the Anchorage Westward Hotel (now Hilton Anchorage) in 1976, and presented slide shows and talks on the Iditarod all around Alaska. Devine drew musher portraits and served on the ITC's board for eight years. In 1979 he volunteered as a checker at Rainy Pass. The 1980 *Iditarod Trail Annual*, published by Page, whose faith in the long race had flowered after its obvious success, praised him for his organizational skills and for meeting deadlines, saying he often offered "Devine guidance."

Promotional material is one of the required items all mushers must carry from Anchorage to Nome. Beginning with the 1974 race, specially designed envelopes, or cachets, commemorating mail delivery by dog team have been part of the racers' gear list; Devine created the first one. The cachets are cancelled in Nome and have become popular collectors items.

Other artists, including Fred Machetanz, who mushed dogs while visiting his uncle Charles Traeger in Unalakleet in the 1930s and painted the image used for each cover of Page's *Iditarod Trail Annual*, Jon Van Zyle, a two-time Iditarod entrant and the official Iditarod artist since 1979, and Charles Gause, who for several years created an Iditarod print for fund-raising purposes, have also contributed time and expertise to race promotion. Van Zyle's yearly posters help support the ITC and bring scenes of the trail to those who can only follow their favorite teams from afar.

The 1970s was the decade of the women behind the men; while male mushers fine-tuned their teams before the race, their wives, girlfriends, or mothers cooked, packaged meals, and sewed dog booties. Page's 1978 *Iditarod Trail Annual* reports Libby Riddles made 300 pairs of booties for Duane (Dewey) Halverson. The future Iditarod champ also prepared his food, "including home-made chili, beef stew, chicken and rice, and other main dishes. She sealed the individual meals in plastic bags so Duane could just toss them in the...pot when he was cooking dog food and he'd have a hot meal right along with the dogs." (In 1985, Halverson placed second, following Riddles into Nome by almost three hours.) Another woman noted in the same issue is Martha Gray, Dick Mackey's mother-in-law, who told Page that for days before the 1977 race started, she and daughter Kathy Mackey "baked, broiled, stewed, and fried complete meals for

him," freezing them in plastic containers. Gray also baked 170 sweet rolls.

Strangers volunteered behind the scenes, too. The U.S. Army helped clear the Iditarod Trail from near Skwentna to McGrath for the inaugural race. Romig Jr. High students paid Rick Swenson's $525 entry fee in 1979 and made 1,200 pairs of dog booties for his team in purple, the school color.

Today's volunteers are just as dedicated, and there are many more of them. ITC Race Director Joanne Potts says

people come out of the woodwork at race time to help; answering phones at race headquarters has been reduced to a four-

Gathered behind a Fred Machetanz painting are Iditarod champions Rick Mackey, Rick Swenson, Dean Osmar, Dick Wilmarth, Dick Mackey, Joe May, Emmitt Peters, Carl Huntington, and Jerry Riley. The mushers came together in Anchorage in 1984 to sign copies of the artist's print to be used as a fund-raiser for the sled dog race. (Jeff Schultz/Alaska Stock)

Volunteer Dianne Herman

March 2002 will be Anchorage resident Dianne Herman's sixth time as a volunteer Iditarod checker at Koyuk, 171 miles east of Nome. Checkers, she says, are the first to arrive at each checkpoint, followed by the "com [communications] person," then veterinarians and race officials. As checker at Koyuk, an Inupiaq community of 297, Herman says the most important aspect is "dealing with the village," meaning things work differently there than they do in the city. Herman ought to know; before her days as an Iditarod volunteer, she spent two years as a teacher in Koyuk. Now, when she flies in every March for the sled dog race, the residents, especially the children, are eager to help her with tasks like hauling water, spreading straw on the snow for the dogs, and scooping the poop.

It takes about two days to set up the checkpoint, Herman says, laughing as she recalls one year when the ITC's boxes of food for race personnel included hot dog buns but no hot dogs. "I take my own food now," she says. "Lot's of salad stuff."

As for sleep, Herman survives on about three hours per night, since one of her duties is checking mushers in and out whenever they reach Koyuk or decide to leave. "It's like one long day!" she says. □

hour shift to give everyone who wants to participate a turn.

As the Iditarod race gathered momentum, offshoots emerged, the most prominent being the Jr. Iditarod. Since 1978 it's been a training ground for future distance mushers. Several teenagers, including Eric Beeman, Karl Clauson, Clarence Shockley, Kenny Pugh, Clint Mayeur, and Rome Gilman, wanted the challenge of a long race, not available in Alaska then for anyone under 18. They met with Redington in 1977 to ask his advice and begin planning. The year

2002 marks the 25th anniversary of the Jr. Iditarod, an approximately 150-mile race from Wasilla to Yentna Station and back. In the race's history, only one girl has won. Christine Delia (now Kriger) of

Family support is a main ingredient in running the Iditarod. Seward musher Dan Seavey gets a hug from his wife as he is called to the starting line; he came in third in the inaugural race, ran again the next year, then took a break until 1997. In 2001, he joined his son and grandson on the trail. (Mark R. Lembersky)

ABOVE: *Officials load $1 bills into a glass case on display throughout the race, symbolizing the prize money. Actual monetary awards are presented as checks. (Richard Montagna)*

ABOVE, RIGHT: *Kimarie Hanson, one of the youngest people to run the Iditarod, packs her sled at the 1998 restart in Willow. She'd previously finished four Jr. Iditarod races. (Tom Bol)*

Skwentna claimed first prize in 1981, running the course in 17 hours, 14 minutes. Kriger recalls intending to race the

Iditarod when she was old enough, until she discovered the costs involved. She no longer mushes, but remembers the best part about racing was "developing good relationships with all the other kids." Jr. Iditarod mushers who've since joined the ranks of their older kin in the 1,049-mile race are Tim Osmar, Lance Mackey, Ray Redington Jr., Aaron Burmeister, and Danny Seavey.

Another offshoot is the Iditasport. An earlier incarnation, founded in 1986 and called the Iditabike, merged in 1991 with the Iditaski, a 125-mile cross-country ski race sponsored by the Iditarod Trail

Blazers. Redington helped get the Iditaski started in 1983, inspired by Mike Salle and Dolly Lefever's 1,000-mile, 43-day ski trip along the Iditarod Trail in 1980. The Iditasport has since evolved into a multi-level competition in which racers choose from four human-powered modes of conveyance — ski, snowshoe, bike, or foot. Held annually, the 100-mile Iditasport in early February covers the

LEFT: *Red, Susan, and Eric Beeman put up a sign for mushers along the south fork of the Kuskokwim River near Farewell Lake, where the family spent the winters of 1974 and 1975. As a teen, Eric was instrumental in organizing the Jr. Iditarod, a mini-version of the long race for ages 14 through 17.* (Marydith Beeman)

ABOVE: *During the race's early years, the pace was slower and competition was not as intense as today. Here, 1974 champion Carl Huntington stops to chat and snack on homemade cookies at the Beeman's trailside "teahouse" near Farewell Lake.* (Marydith Beeman)

first part of the Iditarod Trail from Knik; the week after, racers can choose one of three extensions of the route — the Iditasport 130, from Knik to Finger Lake; the Iditasport Extreme, 350 miles from Knik to McGrath; or the Iditasport Impossible, more than 1,000 miles from Knik to Nome. Rules are few, and contestants are expected to be wilderness and cold-weather savvy. Race Director Dan Bull says all entrants have to pre-qualify for the Extreme, with about 50 entrants, and the Impossible, with about 20; about 80 people enter the shortest race. "Nothing compares," he says, to "doing something human-powered over the Alaska Range" in the winter. Facilities range "from survival situations to plush lodges with gourmet food and fine wine."

The Iron Dog, the third major race to emerge from the reopening of the Iditarod Trail, covers 2,000 miles by snow machine from Wasilla to Nome, then backtracks to Kaltag and follows the Yukon and Tanana Rivers to Fairbanks. It emphasizes stamina and strategies such as whether to drive during the day or at night and where to take mandatory layovers. Twenty or more 55-gallon barrels of fuel must be flown to Puntilla, Rohn, and Ophir, the most remote areas. Winners reach the finish line in about one week.

In the 1980s, the focus of the Iditarod

Trail Sled Dog Race as a male-dominated event shifted to its female champions, Libby Riddles and Susan Butcher. Riddles had finished the Iditarod twice before, placing 18th and 20th, so when she beat everyone else to the finish line in 1985, driving her team through a raging storm, race fans and mushers were surprised. They nevertheless celebrated her victory, even though most had predicted Susan Butcher, a race veteran who'd placed second the year before, would be the first woman to win the race. Butcher, though, was forced to scratch that year after a moose, surprised mid-trail in the dark, stomped repeatedly through her team, killing two and injuring 13 dogs. The media jumped on Riddles's victory, interviewing her, snapping her photo, presenting her to the world, holding her up as a role model to other women. Butcher's triumphs the next three years solidified the image of the Iditarod as a fair race won not necessarily by physical strength, but by the fastest dogs and skilled, dedicated mushers. Two women consecutively winning the Iditarod created a wave of euphoria among women around the nation. A popular slogan appeared on t-shirts, and women, especially Alaskans, gleefully repeated it at every chance: "Alaska: Where Men are Men and Women Win the Iditarod."

Lead dogs Axle and Dugan led Libby Riddles and the rest of her team to Nome during a Norton Sound blizzard in 1985, making her the first woman to win the Iditarod. (Jeff Schultz/Alaska Stock)

LEFT: *For the most part, fuel stoves have replaced open campfires during the race, but occasionally mushers prefer the traditional method. Here, Jeff King, veterinarian Phil Meyer, and Martin Buser heat water to mix with dog food at Cripple, 503 miles from Anchorage. (Jeff Schultz/Alaska Stock)*

ABOVE: *At the 1980 awards banquet in Nome, Joe May of Trapper Creek credited his son and his dog handler with helping him win the Iditarod. He'd also trained his team in "anything but ideal conditions" (mud and ice) near his home, creating strong dogs that didn't balk at the rough trail that year. (Jeff Schultz/ Alaska Stock)*

RIGHT: *Dean Osmar only ran the Iditarod twice, but on his second try, in 1984, he won. His son, Tim, a 16-time Iditarod veteran, came close to victory when he placed third in 1992. Both men live on the Kenai Peninsula and commercial salmon fish in the summer. (Jeff Schultz/Alaska Stock)*

FAR RIGHT: *A wolf ruff keeps Herbie Nayokpuk's face warm while racing. Hundreds of miles of the Iditarod Trail cut across Interior Alaska where temperatures frequently drop below zero, even in March. Nayokpuk is no stranger to stinging snow and storms; his home village of Shishmaref, 126 miles north of Nome, lies exposed to fierce winds blowing in from the Chukchi Sea. (Bill Devine)*

Some Changes

Leading the Way

Breaking and marking the Iditarod Trail has come a long way. In the early years, empty whiskey bottles sat propped in the snow for guidance. Later, bright surveyor's tape tied around tree branches or on wooden tripods led mushers to Nome. The ITC now uses standard Iditarod markers.

Joe Delia recalls breaking trail by snow machine near Skwentna in 1972. "There was bad overflow on some of those lakes," he says. New snow sometimes obliterated trail markers, sending mushers hours out of their way down the wrong path; other times, mushers mistook strands of neon tape marking bush residents' traplines or snow machine trails for Iditarod markers,

ending up at a dead end or cabin miles off course.

In 1983, Dave Monson and Dewey Halverson had just left Shageluk when they had to search for signs of the trail on their hands and knees, feeling for snow machine tracks and peering at twigs to see if sled runners had broken any.

ITC Development Director Greg Bill contrasts those days with modern race preparations, saying, "It's impossible to get lost out there now."

Race Expenses

Footing the bill for the Iditarod Trail Sled Dog Race has always been a

challenge for the ITC. As determined by race officials in the 1970s, the ITC is responsible for many tasks, including a pre-race mushers' banquet, providing communications along the trail during the race, breaking and marking the trail, flying checkers and other volunteers to checkpoints, advertising, and of course, awarding prize money at the end of the race. Expenses have grown over the years from more than $220,000 in 1979 to almost $4 million in 2000.

To help the coffers grow, the ITC began a sweepstakes raffle in 1979; 1,049 tickets at $100 each were offered, 862 sold. First prize was a Piper Super Cub worth

$27,965, and won, ironically, by a pilot. Sharon Hess flew her new plane from Anchorage to her home in Wasilla. Also given away that year were a snow machine, fishing trips, a vacation in Hawaii, and 1,049 bottles of Rainier beer. Big-ticket items like pickup trucks, snow machines, and vacation packages continue to draw raffle customers.

Some mushers got involved early on with fund-raising, giving the proceeds to their chosen organization. In 1979, Jim Lanier, a pathologist at Anchorage's Providence Hospital, earned $14,000 in pledges that he donated to its thermal unit for burn victims.

Sponsorship, the responsibility of each musher who wishes to seek it, plays a more important role now than before. In 1980, sponsors ranged from individuals to local restaurants to outdoor equipment

FACING PAGE: *Juan Alcina's team leaves the starting chute amidst cheers from the crowd. Originally from Spain, the four-time Iditarod finisher now makes his home in Willow. Teams leave two minutes apart; extra time is added as necessary during each musher's mandatory 24-hour layover to compensate. (Tom Bol)*

RIGHT: *Veteran Iditarod musher DeeDee Jonrowe of Willow talks to a TV crew, one of many that cover the Iditarod. Newspaper and radio journalists seek interviews with mushers too, usually at the start, restart, and finish line, but some fly to checkpoints such as Finger Lake, easily accessible by bush plane, or McGrath, with regularly scheduled commercial flights. (Barb Willard)*

stores to national magazines. Huge corporations today sponsor the most successful mushers, some of whom help their backers by appearing in TV or magazine ads.

Mushers in 1975 paid $200 to enter the race; the 2002 entry fee is $1,850. Total expenses of running the race depend on whether a musher owns or rents dogs and gear. Major items like sleds, a four-wheeler for summer training, and a truck with dog boxes, to the hundreds of smaller items such as harnesses, ropes, collars, water buckets, and chains, all add up; months of training and then running the Iditarod can easily top $100,000.

Prize money has grown from a $12,000 first-place award to $68,571. Only places one through 20 won prize money in 1973; now, places one through 30 are considered "in the money," while all other finishers receive up to $1,049, funded by Idita-Rider revenue. Mushers suggested and the ITC initiated the Idita-Rider program in 1995; anyone can bid from $500 to $7,500 to ride in the sled of any musher from Anchorage's starting line to a drop-off point part way through the city. Part of the proceeds go toward a Jr. Iditarod scholarship. According to the ITC, the main reasons for paying all Iditarod finishers is to help mushers

LEFT: *Rick Swenson, left, and Joe Redington draw ITC raffle tickets before the race begins. Many mushers say raising money for support is harder than racing, but most need the extra financial help; sponsor logos appear on clothing, sled bags, and other gear. (Barb Willard)*

BELOW: *Winner of the 1983 Iditarod, Nenana musher Rick Mackey exhibits a frosty mustache and beard, a common sight along the trail during the race. He's run the Iditarod most years since 1975, and has 13 top-10 finishes to his name. (Jeff Schultz/Alaska Stock)*

By Penny Rennick

Iditarod officials stress that the dogs are the heart of the race and that proper care of dogs is paramount, to the officials and to the mushers. But dogs do die, and when they do, debate rages.

Thousands of dogs have run in the official Iditarod races. Out of 850 dogs in the first two races, 30 died, though veterinarians deemed most deaths "not race related." Succeeding years saw fewer and fewer dog deaths and a tightening of regulations about how to deal with deaths. In 1996, a dog in race champion Rick Swenson's team died and the ITC automatically withdrew him under ITC rules then in effect. A later investigation cleared Swenson of any wrongdoing.

But there have been incidents of mistreatment, and another former champion, Jerry Riley, was banned from the race for mistreating dogs. After nearly 10 years out of the race, he was allowed to compete again by a vote of the Iditarod board of directors. Each year, however, he must go before the board to plead his case. Some longtime Iditarod supporters questioned the decision to reinstate Riley, but Rick Koch, president of the board, explains: "Jerry made a fundamental change

in his life. His life is defined by the sport of distance dog racing and as a gesture toward one person by a board of somewhat compassionate people, we felt it was the right thing to do."

Iditarod rules regarding dog treatment also change as new information is learned about dogs and dog care. Formerly, according to Koch, when a dog died, mushers were guilty of mistreatment unless they could prove they were in no way negligent or responsible for the death. "People try to wordsmith rules so a negative specter is not cast on a musher from a dog death. The rule in effect during the Swenson incident was unwieldy and not a good rule. Current rules give officials more latitude to determine if a musher did something wrong."

By far the majority of mushers view the top dogs as professional athletes with whom they stand a chance of earning substantial race prizes and breeding fees for their kennels. But what about the dogs that just don't measure up to racing standards? According to Koch, the answer depends on how the musher manages his or her kennel. Most are responsible. For instance, DeeDee Jonrowe's kennel only produces one or two litters a year. There are no unplanned

Dog Deaths

pregnancies. Dogs that aren't long-distance runners might be sold for middle-distance racing teams. Or the dogs might be given to people who want them for pets or for recreational mushing. Koch says there is a waiting list of people who want culls from famous mushers' teams. Also, Mush with P.R.I.D.E. [see page 36] produces a kennel handbook and operates a certification program for proper kennel management. Koch acknowledges that there are people out there who do not manage their kennels properly and that some dogs may end up being killed. But "these are not Iditarod mushers," he says. The kennels of Iditarod mushers are inspected. "The Iditarod board doesn't want to police mushers any more than we have to, but it is important to us that people in our race operate in ways that are appropriate. We do not tolerate abuse of canine competitors in any fashion. Any abuse will be dealt with in a swift and meaningful way." □

avoid the extra financial burden of getting their team and gear home after the race. Recently, the ITC also started footing the bill home for mushers, along with their dogs and gear, who scratch, preventing any racer who should quit from driving a team past its limit due to the financial burden of dropping out.

Improving Equipment
One of the most radical changes has been in equipment — dog harnesses, sleds, clothing, and other gear. During the 1974 race, Redington had to remove all his dogs' heavy leather harnesses each time they stopped for more than just a quick rest to avoid the sweaty straps

freezing to the dogs' hair and bunching up in hard, uncomfortable ridges beneath them. By 1980, harnesses consisted of lightweight webbing with better padding; today, unless the harnesses get soaked and must be hung to dry, mushers leave them on their dogs throughout the race, allowing more time for feeding and

ABOVE: *The Iditarod race spirit draws people from the warmth of their homes to participate in the Ice Golf Classic in Nome, one of several matches held during race days. (William Foster)*

RIGHT: *Fat Albert, another example of the stocky dogs used for early Iditarod races, shakes owner Rod Perry's hand. Perry ran the first Iditarod, placing 17th. (Bill Devine)*

resting. Light basket or toboggan sleds have replaced long, bulky freight sleds used in the first few Iditarods. The team pulling less weight runs faster. Sled runners have also become more sophisticated over the years, moving from wood to laminates, fiberglass, and aluminum, contributing to a lighter, stronger, faster sled. Photos of Iditarod mushers in the 1970s show some of them wearing jeans and down jackets, not the best combination for wet weather, or wool, warm but heavy after falling through overflow on the trail. Today's array of lightweight, breathable, waterproof garments lets mushers layer according to conditions and move more freely while still remaining warm. When temperatures drop below zero, however, they don the old cold-weather standbys — bunny boots, parkas with fur ruffs, or synthetic snow suits.

Calories Equal Heat
Keeping warm on the trail also requires a lot of calories, and mushers eat foods high in fat, carbohydrates, and protein.

Redington reported that in the late 1970s he ate mostly New York steaks along the trail, fried in butter and cooked "medium" during the first part of the race; the closer he got to Nome, the faster he cooked them and the more "rare" they were. Tang, during those years, was a staple in the Iditarod diet. Riddles, in the mid 1980s, feasted on steaks, pizza, bacon, cheese, trail mix, and *akutaq* ("Eskimo ice cream," made with seal oil, berries, and sugar). With the open camp-fire eventually taking a back seat to compact stoves, mushers started saving time by boiling their own meal-in-a-bag as they heated water for their dogs, easily cooking pre-packaged dishes like pasta with shrimp. Sweets also take center stage in the mushers' bag of goodies. Candy bars, homemade cinnamon rolls, and cake don't seem like indulgences to someone burning up to 10,000 calories a day during the race; electrolyte replacement drinks have become popular too.

Humans aren't the only athletes on the trail that need frequent feedings. In his book, Attla recalls getting lost past McGrath during the 1973 race and nearly running out of dog food. He, Bobby Vent, Dan Seavey, and Dick Wilmarth all teamed up for two days trying to find the trail again. Attla had seen moose tracks a few miles back and suggested they go hunt the animal for food. He and Wilmarth started out in search of it, then heard an airplane circling, so abandoned their idea. The plane landed, and the pilot gave them emergency rations and pointed them in the right direction for the next checkpoint.

Mushers living in Alaska's rural communities have opportunities for amassing subsistence dog food throughout the seasons. Native mushers Rudy Demoski, Herbie Nayokpuk, and Carl Huntington (the only musher to have won the Iditarod and the North American and Fur Rendezvous World Championship Sled Dog Races), fed their dogs the same diet during the Iditarod as they did in their home villages, such as dried fish and

LEFT: *Experienced lead dogs help Robin Jacobson of Minnesota navigate through the Alaska Range's Dalzell Gorge, a place known for its steep hills and ice. Alfred H. Brooks of the USGS named Dalzell Creek in 1902 for a Pennsylvania miner who'd followed its frozen path the previous year. (Jeff Schultz/ Alaska Stock)*

BELOW: *Ruby residents gather to photograph and congratulate Martin Buser (left) as he eats a gourmet dinner, prepared each year at either Ruby (even years) or Anvik for the first musher who reaches the Yukon River. The recipient also gets $3,500. (Jeff Schultz/ Alaska Stock)*

beaver, reducing the chances of the dogs getting sick from a sudden change to commercial food. Today, chances of getting lost on the trail are few, and with the help of the Iditarod Air Force, a fleet of privately owned planes, bags of dog food for each team are flown to checkpoints, ready when the teams arrive.

Today's mushers are bolstered by sponsors and hundreds of volunteers, scrutinized and analyzed by media and thousands of fans worldwide. With improved trail marking, a bigger purse beckoning, better equipment, organized food drops, and humane dog care, winning times have steadily dropped from almost three weeks to just more than nine days. Dick Wilmarth's 1973 victory of 20 days compared to Doug Swingley's record-breaking 2000 time of nine days, 58 minutes, six seconds illustrates and embodies the leaps the Iditarod has made in the past 30 years. What will define the race on its 60th anniversary? ∎

Summer training is no small task. In Birchwood, at Jim Lanier and Anna Bondarenko's kennel, Lanier hooks eager dogs to a towline attached to a four wheeler tied to the fence. Once the dogs are harnessed and clipped in place, the musher opens the gate, starts the ATV, releases it, and hangs on tightly. The dogs lunge forward, and the team races away into a warm afternoon. Lanier and Bondarenko carry a cooler with water for the dogs to drink and small bags of frozen corn to hold briefly on a dog's inner thigh if the dog appears to be overheating. (Susan Beeman, AGS staff)

A Timeline of the Race

1967: Joe Redington's and Dorothy Page's dream of reestablishing the Iditarod Trail comes to life with the 56-mile Centennial Iditarod sled dog race, commemorating the 1867 Alaska Purchase. Winner Isaac Okleasik of Teller takes home $7,000. Leonhard Seppala dies before the race, and his wife, Constance, is special guest of honor in his place at the awards ceremony.

1968: Bad weather foils plans for the second Iditarod race.

1969: The second short Iditarod is held, but only 12 mushers enter, and the entire purse shrinks to $1,000. Sprint musher George Attla wins.

1970-71: Redington and others gather support for a sled dog race from Anchorage to Nome.

1972: The U.S. Army helps Redington, Joe Delia, Dick Mackey, and others clear sections of the Iditarod Trail from near Skwentna, across the Alaska Range, to McGrath in preparation for the first long Iditarod race. Howard Farley in Nome organizes trail clearing from that end.

1973: Thirty-five racers leave the starting line in Anchorage. Redington can't afford to run the race; he stays behind to raise money for the purse. Winner Dick Wilmarth, a miner from Red Devil, 60 miles southeast of the old town of Iditarod, wins $12,000 for first prize (total prize money is $50,000, with the first 20 mushers receiving monetary awards). His lead dog, Hot Foot, gets loose in Nome after the race and disappears; Wilmarth later discovers the husky safely back at Red Devil, almost 500 miles away. In last place after 32 days, five hours, nine minutes, one second, John Schultz of Delta Junction receives the

Only those with official clearance, such as photographers, media personnel, family members, and handlers, are allowed next to the temporary racetrack as teams leave Anchorage. Mitch Seavey of Seward, shown here with an Idita-Rider in the sled basket and a tag sled with handler behind, placed fourth in 1998, winning $33,660. (Tom Bol)

Inupiaq musher Isaac Okleasik beat 58 other mushers to the finish line of the 56-mile Centennial Race in 1967. He used his working dogs, trained to run many miles per day pulling heavy loads. (Bill Devine)

Red Lantern Award, a symbol of tenacity in sled dog racing given to the last-place finisher. The Iditarod Trail Committee begins the practice of reserving bib number one as a symbolic gesture honoring a musher or non-musher who's made a significant contribution to sled dog racing and the Iditarod.

1974: Mary Shields is the first woman to cross the finish line; she and Lolly Medley are the first women to run the race. Redington enters, placing 11th and winning $465. Rookie Carl Huntington wins in 20 days, 15 hours. "Red Fox" Olson arrives in Nome nine days later, winning the Red Lantern Award. Temperatures range from minus 50 degrees Fahrenheit to 43 above throughout the race.

1975: Rookie musher Emmitt Peters ("The Yukon Fox") of Ruby shaves six days off the race record. The original burled arch is constructed, then erected at the finish line in Nome, after Olson's suggestion the race needs something more definite than the previous year's line of Kool-Aid sprinkled on snow and the words "The" and "End" scrawled on two paper plates. Nome Mayor Leo Rasmussen reorganizes the Nome Kennel Club, the oldest dog mushing club in Alaska, which sponsors the first "serum re-run" to commemorate the 50th anniversary of the 1925 effort to bring diphtheria antitoxin to Nome by dog team. Descendants of some of the original relay-mushers participate.

1976: Jerry Riley of Nenana wins the lowest first prize in the history of the Anchorage to Nome race — $7,200. Rick Swenson finishes 10th in his first race.

1977: The Iditarod Trail Sled Dog Race garners international attention; Ian Wooldridge, a sports writer for *The London Daily Mail*, circulation six million, charters a plane to follow the race and write an article. Rick Swenson achieves his first of five victories. The race route begins its alternating pattern of a northern route in even years, a southern route in odd; it's the first time the route passes through Iditarod. Several teenage mushers commence plans for a Jr. Iditarod race.

1978: In the closest call in Iditarod history, Dick Mackey beats Swenson across the finish line by one second. Eleven children and teens each in junior and senior divisions run the first Jr. Iditarod, about 40 miles round-trip near Knik. The ITC is able to begin paying some members of its previously all-volunteer staff. For the first time, women place "in the money": Susan Butcher wins $600 and Varona Thompson, daughter of Iditarod Air Force pilot Larry Thompson, wins $500.

1979: Swenson wins a second victory, making him the first multiple winner in the race's history. Included in the front-runners is Susan

Butcher, the first woman to achieve top-10 status. For the first time, a cash prize, $1,500, is awarded to the Rookie of the Year by the village of St. Michael. A single lightning strike in October 1979 starts a wildfire in what is later called the "Farewell Burn"; 40 miles of Iditarod Trail and several historic roadhouses dating back to the 1910s fall victim to the flames, and fallen trees across the trail in this windy stretch plague mushers for years afterward.

1980: Joe May wins, knocking more than seven hours off Peters's 1975 record. Honorary bib number one is shared for the first time, between Seppala and Wild Bill Shannon, also a driver in the 1925 serum run. A record seven women enter this year's race. The ITC introduces a mandatory one-hour vet check stop at White Mountain. The starting time differential (mushers leave two minutes apart) is compensated for during the required 24-hour layover to provide equal time on the trail for each contestant.

1981: Swenson wins his third Iditarod, setting a new record at 12 days, eight hours, 45 minutes, two seconds. The purse is now at $100,000.

1982: Anchorage station KTVA broadcasts the first live television coverage of the restart. Swenson beats Butcher to the finish line by less than four minutes. Herbie Nayokpuk, nicknamed "The Shishmaref Cannonball" in honor of his hometown and his customary racing speed, finishes 12th despite having had a triple bypass five months earlier.

1983: Rick Mackey, 1978 champion Dick Mackey's son, wins. A record number of mushers, 65, enters the race, now started from down-town Anchorage's Fourth Avenue instead of Mulcahy Park.

1984: Dean Osmar wins. Rookie mushers now must submit proof of successful completion of an ITC-recognized race of at least 200 miles prior to running the Iditarod.

1985: Libby Riddles struggles through a huge storm on the Bering Sea coast to claim victory, becoming the first woman to win the Iditarod. Attacked by a moose, Butcher loses part of her team and is forced to scratch. A storm dumps snow, rain, and freezing rain on the trail, prompting Race Marshal Donna Gentry to put the race on hold three days after the start. Food for all 58 drivers and 810 dogs stranded at Rainy Pass can't be flown in because of bad weather. Some mushers eat dog food due to low supplies of human food. Gentry freezes the race once more a few days later, again because of weather.

1986: Butcher wins her first of three in a row. The new Iditarod headquarters opens in its

Known for his sprint-mushing prowess, George Attla entered the two short Iditarod races, in 1967 and 1969, winning the second one. He managed fourth place in the first long Iditarod from Anchorage to Nome, but scratched the next year and never ran it again. He did, however, continue to succeed in sprint racing. (Bill Devine)

current location; prior to this, ITC meetings were held at the Page's cabin in Wasilla. Seventy-three mushers, the most to date, enter the race. Rune Hesthammer of Norway wins Rookie of the Year Award. Hesthammer finishes 10th.

1987: Butcher wins again. Martin Buser finishes in the top 10 for the first time.

1988: Butcher wins her third race in a row. DeeDee Jonrowe breaks into the top 10 with her sixth Iditarod. Lesley Monk is the only English woman in the race's history to finish.

1989: Joe Runyan of Nenana wins. Rookie Mike Madden of North Pole suffers from salmonella and after being cared for at a makeshift camp by several other mushers, is flown to an Anchorage hospital, where he's treated and recovers. Dorothy G. Page, "Mother of the Iditarod," dies at her home in Wasilla.

After Susan Butcher officially retired from the Iditarod to begin a family, she still kept close ties with the race by reporting from the trail. Here, she uses Charlie Boulding's team at McGrath to demonstrate to a TV crew proper dog care on the trail. (Mark R. Lembersky)

1990: Butcher achieves her fourth victory in five years. Riley is banned from the race for life. At 84, Norman Vaughan is the oldest musher to cross the finish line in the history of the race.

1991: Swenson wins a fifth victory, the only musher with this record. A new Dodge truck is included with the first-place cash prize, becoming a tradition.

1992: Buser wins. Jeff King breaks into the top 10 for the first time in sixth place. Rookie Doug Swingley places ninth. Pressure begins to build from animal rights groups such as PETA (People for the Ethical Treatment of Animals) and the HSUS (Humane Society of the United States) concerning dog deaths during the race and dog culling practices among some mushers. The ITC implements the "corralling" rule: mushers must rest in the same area at checkpoints rather than spread out through the village in private homes. This allows officials to make sure no one is receiving illegal assistance, and makes vet checks more efficient. Mushers organize Mush withP.R.I.D.E.

1993: King wins in 10 days, 15 hours, setting a new record. Redington leads his first "Iditarod Challenge," a mushing tour of the historic trail just after the race, costing participants, who drive their own teams but leave dog care to handlers and enjoy meals cooked by others, a hefty $15,000.

1994: Buser wins. Butcher announces her retirement from the Iditarod after the race. Six mushers suffer carbon monoxide poisoning while napping in an airtight tent heated by propane at the Finger Lake checkpoint. None are seriously injured. Nome resident Aaron Burmeister is the first high school student to run. The ITC incorporates a new rule requiring rookies to submit proof of two qualifying races totaling at least 500 miles, neither of which can be less than 200 miles.

1995: Doug Swingley of Montana is the first non-Alaskan to win, breaking the 10-day race barrier with a final time of nine days, two hours, 42 minutes, 19 seconds and winning a record $52,500. The ITC initiates the Idita-Rider program in which fans bid for the privilege of riding the first few miles through Anchorage in their favorite musher's sled.

1996: King wins. One of Swenson's dogs dies in harness; under ITC rules in effect at the time, the ITC must withdraw him. Controversy surrounding the decision stirs debate about race rules. Long after the race, Swenson is vindicated, the incident serving to refine regulations covering "expired dogs," giving a musher the benefit of the doubt until veterinarians can perform a necropsy to determine the cause of death.

1997: Buser wins the 25th anniversary Iditarod, joining Swenson and Butcher as the only mushers to win the race at least three times. Cash awards are expanded to include mushers arriving 21st or later; each receives $1,049 just for finishing, funded by the Idita-Rider program.

1998: King takes first place. DeeDee Jonrowe comes in second, making this her 11th year in a row as a top-10 finisher, the record for non-champions.

1999: Swingley wins. The original burled arch breaks when volunteers move it off of Nome's Front Street after the race, but is replaced

On the trail near the restart, the Philips family watches live TV coverage of the Iditarod while waiting for teams to pass. Hundreds of spectators come to the trail's edge on the first day of the race to cheer the mushers and dogs. (Barb Willard)

before the next year's race. Joe Redington Sr., "Father of the Iditarod," dies at his Knik home.

2000: Swingley wins again, setting a record of nine days, 58 minutes, six seconds. Anyone crossing the finish line in first through 30th is now considered "in the money," while mushers placing 31st or later receive $1,049 for finishing. Anna Bonderenko of Birchwood is the first Russian woman to run the Iditarod.

2001: Swingley wins once more, catching up to Butcher's four victories. At 47, he is the oldest musher to win. A snow machine crashes into Wasilla musher Mike Nosko's team on the Yentna River, injuring his dogs and forcing him to scratch. Pedro Curuchet is the first Iditarod entrant from South America, Morten Fonseca the first from Denmark. For the first time in Iditarod history, three generations from one family (Dan, Mitch, and Danny Seavey) run in the same race, placing 44th, 42nd, and 43rd, respectively. □

It's About the Dogs

By Mark Weber

EDITOR'S NOTE: *Now an Anchorage resident and Alaska Geographic Society marketing director, Mark used to live in Dillingham where he had a dog team.*

Team members peer from their boxes, surveying the crowd of people and dogs on Anchorage's Fourth Avenue on race day. Each box is padded with straw to keep its occupant warm.
(Tom Bol)

As Doug Swingley's dog team passed through the frigid Nome night and crossed under the burled arch to win the 29th Iditarod Trail Sled Dog Race, he was also in a real sense completing a journey of more than 10,000 years and of countless miles.

It was 10 or a dozen millennia ago that the first bonds began to form between humans and canids, the genus that includes dogs and wolves. This was soon after the last ice age, when people began to live in permanent settlements. Those early canids might have been wolves or wolf-like wild dogs, similar to the Eurasian wolf, which was smaller than the Arctic wolf. The canids would have become familiar with the efficiency of the humans as hunters and gatherers and the scraps of food available near their habitations. The humans might have realized that the canids behaved as an extra set of far more perceptive senses to warn of danger, take note of nearby game, and fill lonely hours. Dogs and humans were able to easily accommodate each other in part because the social organization of canids and humans is much the same. The behavior of both is oriented toward groups. Both have developed an elaborate set of expressions, vocalizations, and actions to convey needs, and to signal group affiliation and standing within that group. Wolves, like humans, hunted cooperatively to bring down large game.

Initially, dogs' roles were as companion, guard, hunter, and herder. In Alaska, experts think humans first hitched dogs to pull sleds about 1,500 years ago. Dog mushing was well established among the Eskimos of North America when the first white explorers arrived. It became apparent to anyone trying to move freight in Alaska after the waterways froze for the season that dogs were ideally adapted for winter travel. Deep snow, narrow trails, and icy slopes were formidable barriers for horses, oxen, or other traditional draft animals. In winter they required expensive hay or grain. Dogs, on the other hand, could traverse almost any terrain that a human could. Joe Redington and Susan Butcher have even driven a dog team to the summit of Mt. McKinley, North America's tallest peak. Dogs could be fed off the land with the same provisions as humans: fish, caribou, moose, and small game. According to the Iditarod Trail Committee, pound for pound, sled dogs are the most powerful draft animals on Earth. Raymond and Lorna Coppinger in their book *Dogs: A Startling New Understanding of Canine Origin, Behavior and Evolution* (2001) demonstrate that dogs are also the fastest animals on Earth over distances of more than 10 miles.

At the turn of the twentieth century assorted native breeds, including village dogs, malamutes, McKenzie River huskies, and even wolves, mixed with a variety of dogs imported from the Lower 48, were in use. Trappers, freight mushers, and mail carriers needed strong, heavy dogs able to break trail, pull huge loads of freight, sleep in the snow, and withstand wind and extreme cold. Commonly, teams of 20 or more dogs pulled long sleds with a half-ton or more of cargo.

When miners, trappers, and Natives gathered in towns and villages they naturally compared the quality of their teams and organized races. In the early 1900s, the All-Alaska Sweepstakes was the most prestigious of these events. Some mushers began to develop teams for racing, not just work. When a Russian trader brought the first Siberian husky to Alaska in 1908, mushers were impressed with the relatively small, tough animals and the next year, Fox Maule Ramsay, a Nome miner, bought 60 Siberians from the Chukchi Eskimos. His teams won first, second, and fourth places in the 1910 All-Alaska Sweepstakes. Leonhard Seppala achieved fame using Siberian huskies to win the Sweepstakes in 1915, 1916, and 1917, and also used them in the 1925 Serum Run. The Siberians gained additional popularity when Seppala

entered them in races along the U.S. East Coast.

As planes took over mail and supply routes after WWI, use of dog teams for work declined rapidly. Snow machines, introduced in the 1960s, contributed to their demise as owners weighed the practicality of caring for and feeding a team for 12 months when they were only used for seven months of the year.

Though the number of actual working teams dwindled, dog races still regularly took place. At this point racing was almost entirely sprinting, usually heats of about 20 miles taking place on two or three consecutive days. Breeders developed dogs to specialize in running at top speed over a short course. Certain kennels and villages built reputations for producing outstanding dogs. Gareth Wright and his Aurora Huskies developed a racing dynasty that is still a force today. George Attla became a legend as a racer and breeder.

Puppies at Vern Halter's kennel in Willow chow down in a mass feeding. Good nutrition, lots of exercise, and socialization at an early age influence a dog's chance at being chosen for an Iditarod team. Halter has run the race 14 times since 1983, with a strong team pulling him across the finish line in 1999 in third place. (Barb Willard)

RIGHT: *Vern Halter prepares frozen squares of high fat meat, usually beaver, but often moose, fish, or fish heads, a mixture made before the Iditarod race starts. Measuring meal portions correctly is important, and each musher must estimate how much dog food to send ahead to checkpoints. (Barb Willard)*

FAR RIGHT: *Roamer, Joe Redington's famous dog with a barrel chest, an excellent attribute for a distance dog, was born in 1960 and lived 15 years. He sired many puppies while at the musher's kennel and Redington thought him the finest dog he ever owned. Some dogs from Roamer's bloodline, such as Feets, Andy, Granite, Dugan, and Axle helped other racers triumph in the Iditarod. He's seen here shedding his woolly undercoat. (Bill Devine)*

The first Iditarods were dominated by Native mushers whose families had generations of experience with dogs and who knew how to camp out in the wilderness and live off the land. There were no dogs bred specifically for long-distance racing because for years there had been no long-distance races. Mushers used their sprint dogs or working dogs and adjusted training and nutrition to accommodate the rigors of long-distance travel

Carl Huntington, winner of the second Iditarod, used some of the dogs from that team to later win the world's fastest sprint race, the North American Championship in Fairbanks. Dogs show considerable flexibility depending on training and disposition and though it is not common, the same dog may, at different times, participate successfully in sprint racing and distance racing, and may also be a family pet.

In his book, *The Secrets of Long Distance Training and Racing* (1987), five-time Iditarod champion Rick Swenson provided his view of the importance of good dogs in racing: "…I don't care what anybody else says, the dog is the number one athlete. Without the dogs, no matter how good the driver is, he or she is not going to win."

Dog breeders use the same principles of animal husbandry practiced for thousands of years by others engaged in the breeding of domesticated animals. At its simplest, animals are bred for selected traits. Dogs with desirable traits are bred to other dogs with that trait and dogs with undesirable traits or behaviors are not bred or are culled. Though purebred Siberian huskies have raced in the Iditarod, virtually all dogs on competitive teams today are "mutts." Mushers continually experiment by introducing traits from breeds other than traditional northern sled dogs. For example, hounds have been admired for centuries for their toughness, intelligence, and good feet. Their influence is now well established in racing and many dogs sport floppy ears rather than the traditional erect pointed ears of the Arctic breeds. Iditarod champion Doug Swingley, on the other hand, says he's never crossed hound into his line though he has mixed in "houndy-looking" huskies.

The dog racing world has recently been astounded by the success of Swedish musher Egil Ellis and his breed of huskies crossed with German and English short-hair pointers. Ellis has been all but unbeatable in the Anchorage and Fairbanks sprint races, winning in record times. However, racing sled dogs is a complex endeavor with many variables and Joe Redington for one thought that the pointer crosses are only part of the equation. "Everyone says it's pointers and all that, but he's a very good dog man," Redington said in a *Mushing* magazine interview. "There's more to it than the dogs. I think he's taught us what sprint racing is all about." Nevertheless, Ellis's success will no doubt cause Iditarod racers to give the bird dogs a second look. Legendary dog breeder Gareth Wright has experimented with pointer-husky crosses and said he thought his dogs would be competitive with Ellis's and would also be competitive in distance racing because they have been bred to have a thicker coat.

Ellis himself has indicated his search for other challenges in the dog racing world may one day include the Iditarod. "Something I've been following for years," Ellis says of the race. "I have deep respect for the mushers in the Iditarod. It's just fascinating to me how they travel that long over that distance…. It will be a few years. We have the dogs, but they don't have the coat for it."

Mushers raise many of their own dogs but they also buy and trade for dogs from other kennels to prevent a loss of vigor due to inbreeding. Good dogs for a competitive Iditarod team might cost upwards of $2,000 and a fine leader may be worth $7,000 - $10,000 or more. Mushers often lease one or more experienced dogs to round out their teams and sometimes a musher, not having the time or space to raise his own dogs, will lease a whole team for a season or a single race.

The alchemy of dog breeding is a favorite topic among mushers and there are almost as many breeding strategies as there are kennels. This is apparent walking down Fourth Avenue in Anchorage on the first Saturday in March. There are a remarkable variety of sizes, colors, and conformations in the dogs preparing to run the Last Great Race. Racers have even finished the Iditarod with dogs entirely from the dog pound.

The ITC allows only "northern dog breeds suitable for arctic travel" to enter the race to ensure that the animals have the coat and other attributes necessary to withstand the extremes of climate found on the trail. Iditarod dogs are generally about 40 to 50 pounds and have the lean, leggy look of marathon runners.

Like all sports, dog mushing boasts its celebrities, and dogs as well as humans are household names in Alaska. Many of Joe Redington's dogs were descen-

Fleece booties prevent dogs' feet from accumulating balls of icy snow between the pads during the Iditarod Trail Sled Dog Race. Velcro strips at the top allow mushers to adjust each bootie precisely. (Jeff Schultz/ Alaska Stock)

dants of Roamer, whom Joe called the best dog he ever had. Roamer was also the father of Joe's lead dog, Feets, and he was the grandfather of Andy, who was key to Rick Swenson's wins in four races and also led Sonny Lindner to victory in the Yukon Quest. Andy was also part of Kathy Swenson's team when she won the European Alpirod. In addition, Roamer was grandfather of Granite, Susan Butcher's indefatigable leader and was great-grandfather of Dugan and Axle, who led Libby Riddles to her victory in 1985. Other canine heroes were D2, Martin Buser's main leader for years and Nugget, who propelled Emmitt Peters's team for 12 years, saved his life twice, and led two Iditarod teams to victory.

Besides breeding, training is the other essential component of successful racing kennels. Corporate sponsorships have enabled some of the top mushers to devote all their time to developing their teams but many mushers still have to secure income by working at other jobs in the off season.

Training aims to develop in dogs the stamina, conditioning, and attitude to run the Iditarod's 1,049 miles and the speed to do it with a winning time.

Seward musher Mark Lindstrom's team races through Anchorage on the first day of the Iditarod. The rope parallel to and between the dogs is called the towline, a neckline is clipped to each dog's collar, and the tug-line runs from the back of each dog's harness to the towline. A slack tugline is evidence that a dog isn't pulling its weight. (Jeff Schultz/Alaska Stock)

Iditarod dogs trot at 10 to 14 miles per hour on a good trail and they do it for more than 100 miles per day. Dog teams may have several thousand miles on the trail by the time they step up to the starting line. Top mushers commonly have a handler run a "puppy team" of young dogs in the Iditarod whose goal is to give the dogs experience and to test the individual dogs over long distances without the intense competitive pressure of the winning teams.

In the snowless seasons, ATVs are often used to run teams on gravel roads and dirt trails. Some mushers employ a kind of doggie carousel which exercises a number of dogs at once. These devices may be motorized and can be used to build up a dog's pace. However, because they only go round and round in a circle they are used more for exercise than for putting serious miles on the team. Mushers have taken advantage of Alaska's reputation as a summer tourist destination to make money as well as to keep their dogs in shape. Linwood Fiedler has developed a business near Juneau where tourists are helicoptered to a glacier for dog sled rides all summer.

Advances in dog nutrition are a significant reason behind the increases in dog performance over the years. Racing dogs may consume more than 10,000 calories while running over 100 miles a day pulling nearly their own weight and also burning energy to keep warm at rest stops. Initially, mushers fed their teams traditional foods based on what was available. When dog racing became a higher profile sport, dog food companies began to get involved as sponsors and put serious effort into understanding dog physiology under racing conditions. Also, as years of experience accumulated, mushers had a large amount of data available to plan their nutrition strategies. The Alaska Dog Mushers Association's International Sleddog Symposium held in Fairbanks each fall as well as other events throughout the Lower 48 states are effective clearinghouses for up-to-date information on recent research.

Dog mushing is a game of feet and mushers pay

extraordinary attention to the condition of their dogs' pads, nails, toes and wrists. Racing dogs are bred to have tough feet but various trail conditions may require additional protection. Mushers check their dogs' feet often during the race because a minor injury can quickly become worse if not taken care of. While running, dog drivers pay close attention to each dog's gait and can quickly sense a problem by a slight change in the pattern of motion of the dozens of feet pulling the sled. Racers are required to carry booties in their sled and may use a thousand or more during a race. The sock-like booties are made from various materials. Today, a fleece material that is lightweight and dries fast is often used. The bootie is secured with a strip of Velcro, a big time-saver from the days when each bootie was tied or taped on. Mushers also employ a variety of ointments. Some of them are off the shelf and some are custom mixtures formulated to treat the nicks, cuts, and swelling dogs' feet may acquire.

Veterinarians staff every checkpoint and examine every dog when a team checks in. They have also been known to stitch up or otherwise treat humans suffering injuries on the trail. Interestingly, there are no rules mandating health exams, nutritional requirements, or rest for the mushers. Drivers are restricted from using illegal drugs or excessive alcohol and the ITC can require a drug test at any time during the race.

The ITC also has rules about prohibited substances for dogs and so far none has been disqualified for drug use. Most testing is done by urinalysis and takes place at several unannounced points in the race as well as before the start and after the finish by an organization independent of the ITC. Because of the complexities of developing a drug strategy for a whole team of dogs over a 10- to 14-day race, it is commonly believed that the pharmacology is too difficult for mushers to successfully attempt.

Mushers are drawn to the Iditarod for a number of reasons, the arduous journey as personal test, the

profound wilderness experience, and the camaraderie of the trail, but for many if not most, it is about the dogs. "The love of the dogs keeps me in it," Swingley said after he finished the unusually difficult 2001 Iditarod. At the starting line on Fourth Avenue in Anchorage or in the final windblown stretch of the trail out of Safety, no one knows what the dogs are "thinking" but their passion is unmistakable. What drives this group of dogs and humans to work together is not hunger or a need to protect territory. According to the Coppingers, "Sled dogs are running because other dogs are running. They are motivated by something the animal behaviorists call social facilitation. There is a rhythm to their run and they can hear that rhythm and they run to it. When you stand on the back of a sled, you can feel it. It is powerful." □

Iditarod dogs live and train outside year-round and are bred to grow a thick layer of woolly fur beneath longer guard hairs; when sleeping on the snow, even during a storm, this insulation system keeps them warm. (Barb Willard)

Today's Iditarod Trail Sled Dog Race

Mush!

Since its official beginning in 1973, the Iditarod Trail Sled Dog Race has grown from 35 entrants to 86 in 2001. Most make it to the finish line, but every year, a handful of mushers scratches, or drops out of the race. Many of them are back at the starting line 12 months later for another chance at competing in what Joe Redington called "one of the greatest sports in the world." That tenacity, that desire to keep trying, is the hallmark of mushers and dogs in this long-distance race. Winning, or even placing in the top 10, nets those mushers thousands of dollars in prize money and hero-status for a time, but that's not why most people enter. They enter because they love to mush and because they love the challenge of wilderness.

The race begins in Anchorage, Alaska's largest city, the state's center of communications and commerce. Thousands of locals and visitors line temporary fences along Fourth Avenue and other streets, snapping pictures of DeeDee Jonrowe, Linwood Fiedler, Paul Gebhardt, Charlie Boulding, Ramy Brooks, Mitch Seavey, Vern Halter, John Baker, Mike Williams, and other bibbed racers waving to the crowd and streaking past, riding sled runners over snow the city hauls in by the truckload. These snow lanes, buffered by berms, snake through downtown. Most winters, natural snowcover pads the rest of the trail.

Dog handlers are invaluable to mushers; one is required to accompany each musher out of Anchorage, usually on a "tag sled" ridden behind the musher's sled. This adds weight and slows the eager dogs as they lunge from the starting line. Sometimes the pair forgoes a tag sled, with the handler riding on the main sled instead.

Vehicle traffic near the race route is either rerouted or closely monitored by crossing guards, and several places along the route offer good vantage points for fans to watch and cheer. The route passes an eclectic range of urban features, including pedestrian culverts and bridges, main roads, a military reserve, a golf course, a correctional center, and a campground before reaching the first official checkpoint at the Eagle River VFW Post.

The Anchorage start gives thousands of spectators a chance to see Iditarod dogs in action, but the teams run only 20 miles before mushers load dogs back into specially designed boxes on the back of pickup trucks and drive another 29 miles to Wasilla, bypassing Knik Arm's open water and the windblown Palmer Flats. During the early years of the race, mushers continued by sled from Eagle River to Knik, crossing the swift Knik River on the two-lane Glenn Highway bridge; due to an increase in traffic between Anchorage and Wasilla in the late 1970s and early 1980s, the bridge was upgraded, increasing traffic speed and creating hazardous conditions for

FACING PAGE: *Teams cluster at the Finger Lake checkpoint, 174 miles from Wasilla; most mushers spend their first night on the trail here. (Fred Hirschmann)*

dog teams. The state Department of Transportation would no longer issue permits allowing teams to cross the bridge, so in characteristic Iditarod spirit, the ITC adopted a new race procedure — mushers unhooked their teams in Eagle River and drove to the restart in Wasilla

A "dog walker" helps racing dogs stay in shape during summer at Susan Butcher's kennel northwest of Fairbanks. The four-time Iditarod champion supervises from the center. (Jeff Schultz/Alaska Stock)

the same day. Now, however, no time is kept during the first day's run, and mushers are treated to stew and cornbread inside the VFW Post at the Eagle River checkpoint. It's a chance for the media to conduct interviews and mushers to socialize. Competitors spend the night at home or camped out at a friend's house or near Wasilla, performing last-minute adjustments of sleds, towlines (the main line attaching dogs to the sled), and outdoor gear or hoping for one last night of peaceful sleep before the race officially restarts Sunday morning and the clock

begins ticking. Occasionally, as in 2001, lack of snow in the Wasilla area forces the restart to Willow, 20 miles northwest, also accessible by the Parks Highway.

Leaving Wasilla at two-minute intervals in the same order as the previous day, each team receives a second enthusiastic send-off by family, friends, and fans, some of whom fly thousands of miles just to witness the Iditarod firsthand. Wasilla is an urban wilderness, and mushers take care along this stretch to avoid colliding with errant snow machiners, skiers, and even other dog teams not associated with the Iditarod race. Hordes of spectators gather at various points beside the trail, much of it accessible by the Knik-Goose Bay Road. Not until it reaches Knik, 63 miles from the Anchorage starting line, does the Iditarod Trail leave the road system behind and begin to enter Alaska's wilderness.

Wilderness in Southcentral Alaska, however, does not necessarily mean no one lives there, and nowhere along the route is this more apparent than the section between Knik and Skwentna. Bush planes buzz overhead. Recreational snow machiners roar through forests on the Iditarod Trail and tracks of their own making, packing ruts and moguls into the snow and sometimes driving at excessive speeds. Homesteads and cabins dot the lakes, and inhabitants keep vigil beside the Iditarod Trail during the early part of the race. But with each mile gained, mushers and dogs move farther into Alaska's wild lands and dig deeper into their own reserves of endurance, experience, and skill.

Race Rules

To qualify for the Iditarod Trail Sled Dog Race, mushers must meet several conditions. The ITC considers only those 18 years or older by the starting date and reviews musher performance in pre-qualifying races when considering applications by rookies, mushers who've not completed a previous Iditarod. Each person must enter a race application with the ITC and pay $1,850 to cover ITC and Mush with P.R.I.D.E. membership dues.

Once officially entered, mushers spend the months leading up to the race training hard and organizing pre-race activities: securing sponsors; testing and retesting sleds, harnesses, parkas, and other gear; having each dog checked by a race veterinarian (includes implantation of identification microchips, electrocardiograms or EKGs, vaccinations, and blood work); and buying and shipping dog food to checkpoints.

Strict rules govern the race. The number of dogs required for each team at the beginning is between 12 and 16, and at least half must be on the towline at the end. None may be added during the race. Three mandatory stops are required: a 24-hour layover anywhere along the trail, usually taken at Rohn, Nikolai, McGrath, or Takotna; and two eight-hour rests, one at a Yukon River checkpoint and one at White Mountain, 77 miles from Nome. None of these stops can be combined. Required gear includes sleeping bag, snowshoes, dog booties, ax, cooker and pot for dog food, any promotional material provided by the

ITC, and a record of vet checks along the way; these items must all be carried in an approved sled for the duration of the race. Mushers add personal touches to this list, from energy bars to rifles. Emergency food for themselves and their teams and changes of clothes round out the load. Other rules pertaining to the health of the dogs must also be adhered to, or mushers face disqualification.

The People

Hundreds of people make the race possible. Mushers, of course, are the most

Reaching Rainy Pass in a whiteout, Danny Seavey rides over a rocky section of trail during the 2001 Iditarod, his first time on the trail. The trail rises more than 1,000 feet in only a few miles between the checkpoint at Puntilla Lake and the pass. (Jeff Schultz/Alaska Stock)

visible to the public, with media attention contributing to their exposure. Volunteers, often called the "unsung heroes," are scattered along the trail too, with roles as diverse as pilot, veterinarian, or checker. Many villagers at checkpoints

LEFT: *Downtown Anchorage begins transforming from city streets to sled dog racing avenues a day or two before the race. Dump trucks bring loads of snow to Fourth Avenue, plows disperse it evenly and where needed, and volunteers unroll fencing along sidewalk edges to keep spectators off the track. (Jeff Schultz/ Alaska Stock)*

ABOVE: *Leo Rasmussen, mayor of Nome and longtime Iditarod supporter, visits Anchorage in 1997 to help cheer for teams at the starting line. As volunteer checker at Nome for many years, he says his claim to fame is having checked in 899 of the 1,330 mushers to cross the finish line. (Jeff Schultz/Alaska Stock)*

also pitch in, cooking food, hauling water in buckets from a nearby hole in river or lake ice to the checkpoint building, and giving other volunteers rides around town via all-terrain vehicle (ATV) or snow machine. Supporting and organizing the race is the ITC. Fans, of course, help keep the spirit of the Iditarod alive.

Iditarod mushers come from all walks of life: fishermen, writers, bush pilots; men and women; Alaska Natives and non-Natives; most live in Alaska, but foreign entrants come from France, Norway, Russia, England, Japan, and many other countries. There are full-time mushers who spend summers raising pups and training their teams with a wheeled cart or ATV, winters entering races shorter than the Iditarod, and all year honing their speed, endurance, and wilderness survival skills. Most who are able to pursue the sport year-round do so with the help of sponsors and spouses, but the majority of Iditarod entrants balance mushing with family and job, training and racing part-time, primarily for fun and adventure. Of the hundreds of people who've run the Iditarod since its inception, 23 have completed it 10 times or more; of those, seven have won. All mush for the love of the sport, for even the winner of the Iditarod returns home to mortgage payments and credit card bills. And then there's the cost of running a kennel: dog food and vet care and vehicle maintenance.

Volunteer Coordinator Cheryl Church

estimates between 1,700 and 1,800 people sign on as official Iditarod volunteers every year. Her full-time position

BELOW: *John Barron is an expert in outdoor living. He entered the Iditarod every year except one between 1979 and 2001. Here, he dips water from a hole chopped in Finger Lake. (Jeff Schultz/Alaska Stock)*

RIGHT: *Volunteer trailbreakers set official markers into snow beside the Iditarod Trail near White Mountain, east of Nome. The stakes are four feet long with reflective tape at the top end so they are visible by headlamp. Locals traveling between villages keep much of the route open before the race begins. (Jeff Schultz/Alaska Stock)*

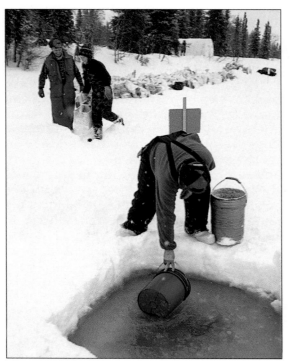

with the ITC is unpaid too; she also works as a full-time surgical technician at the Alaska Native Medical Center. Some volunteers start work long before the race begins. In early February 2001 for example, 1,500 bales of straw, used as dog bedding at checkpoints, had to be bagged, labeled, mailed from Anchorage, and unloaded at villages along the route. Normally, the U.S. Postal Service handles most of the compressed bales, while volunteer bush pilots with the Iditarod Air Force fly the remaining 27,500 pounds of straw to remote checkpoints

lacking mail service, such as Rainy Pass, Eagle Island, and Rohn. The Iditarod Air Force also delivers bags of dog food, extra sleds, human food, and race personnel to many places along the trail. Each musher has about 2,500 pounds of dog food flown to checkpoints; with approximately 70 mushers entering, that's 175,000 pounds. The pilots also ferry dropped dogs back to Anchorage, where volunteers take the animals to the Eagle River Correctional Center; there, inmates feed, water, and care for the canines until their owners return from

the trail. The ITC provides all of the needed supplies.

Pre-race veterinary exams must be performed within two weeks before the start of the race on each dog entered, giving mushers a chance to select the healthiest dogs for their Iditarod team. Vets check heart rates and weight, and inspect paws, eyes, ears, nose, mouth, skin, and joints to determine overall condition. EKGs offer additional information about each animal's heart; only strong, healthy dogs are allowed to race. Vets may at any time between the pre-race exam and six hours after the team has reached Nome request an impromptu blood or urine sample for any dog. This discourages mushers from using prohibited substances such as steroids, anti-inflammatory drugs, and cough suppressants on their dogs. In addition to supervising, vets are there to advise mushers and help keep the dogs healthy, an obvious benefit to racers who care about their teams and the reputation of the race. Stationed along the trail at checkpoints, veterinarians play an impor-

Iditarod Air Force Pilots

Volunteer Iditarod Air Force pilot Richard Dowling gets ready to fly dropped dogs from McGrath back to Anchorage in his Cessna 185. He's helped with the race since 1994. Fights between dogs inside a small plane are rare, as most mushers do not keep aggressive animals for their teams. (Jeff Schultz/Alaska Stock)

In the third week of February, chief volunteer Iditarod Air Force pilot Joe Pendergrass of Wasilla starts hauling straw and dog food to checkpoints. A day or two before the race begins, he straps checkers, veterinarians, and race officials into seats in his Cessna 180 and flies them to race locations. He especially likes taking people who've never been to Alaska or to remote checkpoints. "They're so inspired," he says, "so enthused."

Pendergrass was aware of the Iditarod Air Force long before he became a volunteer pilot. He never had time for the event until he retired. A volunteer pilot must have at least 500 hours of Alaska flying time, he notes. "We're always fightin' the weather," he explains. They fly by VFR, visual flight rules. Turbulence and weather coming down quickly are the two main dangers for pilots.

Anchorage's Bill Mayer, another long-time Iditarod Air Force pilot, remembers what Race Manager Jack Niggemyer said when preparing the pilots before the Iditarod one year: "Guys, one thing. Don't get hurt. It's only a dog race."

If dropped dogs are still tired when flown back to Anchorage, they usually remain calm inside the small planes, but if they've had a chance to rest, they can get excited. Nine dogs can fit into Pendergrass's plane. Two cables are attached to the floor of his aircraft, and each dog is snapped to one to prevent them moving around. Mayer says if dogs begin fighting in his plane, he bounces the tail if he's still on the ground; if he's in the air, he dips the plane sharply up or down, startling the aggressors into submission.

"It's a magical couple of weeks," says Mayer. "It gives you an excuse to fly your own airplane with a purpose." □

ABOVE: *Urine samples are just one method of testing Iditarod dogs for illegal drugs. They can also help diagnose any illness a dog may have contracted, though veterinarians examine every dog before allowing them into the race to assure they are healthy. (Barb Willard)*

ABOVE, RIGHT: *Sixteen dogs pull Big Lake musher Ramey Smyth through the Alaska Range. The two dogs in front are called lead dogs; just behind them are the point or swing dogs. The rest of the group is made up of team dogs, except for those directly in front of the sled, the wheel dogs. Switching dogs to different positions sometimes helps a team run more smoothly. (Jeff Schultz/Alaska Stock)*

tant role during the check-in procedure, including inspection of each dog for signs of injury, fatigue, hyperthermia, or sore feet, and sign each musher's veterinary logbook at every checkpoint. Anchorage veterinarian Dr. Bob Sept says vets "must apply to become an Iditarod vet."

Checkers, hardy souls keeping odd hours during the Iditarod race, sign in each racer at the checkpoint, recording the mushers' official arrival and departure times. In sometimes bitter cold, often in the dark, checkers also examine sled contents for mandatory equipment. In larger communities like McGrath or Unalakleet, checkers frequently appoint their own volunteer helpers.

Without media coverage, the Iditarod wouldn't be the success it is today. Photographers now flock to the start, restart, finish line, and the more easily accessible checkpoints to shoot roll after roll of lead dogs loping around corners, pink tongues flying; teams resting on straw spread over snow; mushers power-

napping with their boots still on. Rick Swenson remembers once, in the race's early years, someone woke him to ask permission to photograph him napping. Experienced media crews today get their pictures or interviews and move aside to make room for others. Some, like Jeff Schultz, the official Iditarod photographer since 1982, have become friends with veteran mushers and race officials; he's gained an insider's look at race life on the Iditarod Trail.

Dangers of the Trail

Despite its urban start, its modern communications systems, and all its safety precautions, some dangers are inherent in the race because of the trail's remoteness. Accidents happen — broken sleds, scraped knees and elbows, smashed noses, temporarily losing the team — all mushers are braced for these incidents from the start. The unforeseen events are the ones that worry them.

Illness can strike a musher anywhere on the trail, and doctors aren't available in many checkpoints. In 1989, Mike Madden, who'd accidentally slashed his finger with his ax and gotten three stitches in McGrath, later began feeling weak as he and his team navigated the trail between Ophir and Iditarod, a lonely 90-mile span. When he stopped to rest

French club members at the McGrath checkpoint offer a café menu to help raise money for a school trip. Their customers include mushers, journalists, visitors, and locals. (Richard Montagna)

Careful not to slip, Rick Swenson straightens his team on a lake near Shaktoolik, the second checkpoint along the Norton Sound coast. Wind blows constantly here, creating icy patches, snowdrifts, and whiteouts. (Jeff Schultz/Alaska Stock)

and feed his dogs, his vision began blurring and a fever overwhelmed him. He collapsed in the snow shortly afterward. Fortunately, another musher was traveling with him; also a rookie, Jamie Nelson recognized the gravity of Madden's

situation. Shortly after she built a fire and set up a make-shift camp, three more rookies arrived — Kathy Halverson, Linwood Fiedler, and Mitch Brazin. Madden, they guessed, could be suffering from hypothermia or blood poisoning

from the earlier injury; he was starting to shout nonsense in his delirium. Jerry Austin joined the group, and he and Fiedler decided to make a dash to Iditarod and alert officials. Bernie Willis, another rookie, stopped just before dawn to help the other exhausted mushers keep watch over Madden, keeping him warm and forcing him to drink liquids. Joanne Potts of the ITC remembers spending "all night [via ham radio] trying to get a helicopter out there," with no luck. At daybreak, the Iditarod Air Force was able to rescue the musher and fly him to Anchorage where doctors successfully treated him for salmonella poisoning. No one has died while running the Iditarod, but Madden came close.

Animal attacks are another hazard mushers face on the trail, as Susan Butcher learned in 1985 when she rounded a corner in the dark to find a moose standing its ground. After stomping two of her dogs to death and injuring 13 others, the moose still did not back down. Dewey Halverson caught up to the distressed team and shot the moose, killing it and ending the attack. Race rules dictate that any game animal such as moose, caribou, or bison killed in defense of life or property must be gutted and the incident reported at the next checkpoint; the meat is then salvaged by locals. A small bison herd thrives in the Farewell area; at one ton, a bison can be a formidable foe. Rather than aggressors, though, these animals are mostly considered welcome residents in the wild country of the Iditarod Trail.

Mushers expect to race through inclement weather during the Iditarod, but sometimes storms prove too fierce to face; other times, unseasonably warm weather hampers progress. In 1985, Race Marshal Donna Gentry "froze" the race twice due to bad weather, concerned for the mushers' and dogs' lives if they continued and because supplies were low at some checkpoints and no airplanes could fly. Audra Forsgren, the checker that year at Ophir, where several mushers waited out the storm, wrote in her race notes, "Weather awful. Pilots can't get anywhere. Had people drying clothes everywhere and sleeping in the sauna, annex, gas house, wood shed, and Denise's [her daughter's] old play house across the road…. There's 323 dogs in the yard." That was also the year Libby Riddles drove her team through a

Martin Buser signs autographs for children at the Unalakleet checkpoint, the first Norton Sound community along the Iditarod Trail. At more than 800 miles from Anchorage, the front-runners are sometimes suffering from lack of sleep by the time they reach the coast. (Jeff Schultz/Alaska Stock)

Norton Sound blizzard to reach Nome, becoming the Iditarod's first female winner. The danger of frostbite, too, looms large for mushers; extra pairs of dry socks and gloves or mittens take up space in every sled. For dogs with sparse belly fur — some males but especially females whose fur didn't grow back after having pups — mushers carry flank protectors that keep exposed skin from freezing. Warm weather can also slow teams and create difficult mushing conditions. Martin Buser, recalling the trail between Rainy Pass and Nikolai in 2001, mentions glare ice, bare ground, and dust being kicked up by his dogs' feet while traversing the "buffalo tunnel" of the Farewell Burn, a notoriously windy stretch lined with stunted spruces.

Even veteran mushers tell stories of losing their team in a storm after snowshoeing ahead to break trail or after hitting a tree and being thrown from the sled. Joe Redington drove a team of young adult dogs in the 1992 Iditarod; near Finger Lake, the pups tore off the trail, throwing the musher off the sled. The dogs ran back to the trail and kept going despite Redington's shouts. He began walking, sweating with the exertion even in the minus-30 degree cold, a perilous situation, for he couldn't stop moving or he'd freeze to death. He refused a ride from fellow contestant Mike Williams, but Williams later caught up to the wayward team and tied it to a tree. Redington eventually joined his dogs and spent a miserable night trying to stay warm. The next day, the dogs lunged again, dumping Redington headfirst into a creek. He walked two miles to the Rainy Pass checkpoint. His dogs were there, but it had been a tough stretch.

There's No Place Like Nome

Nome comes alive every March as Iditarod mushers push toward the finish line. Residents emerge from a cocoon of winter; visitors fly in and book up every bed in town to see their favorite mushers run under the burled arch. From book

signings to basketball tournaments, the town's calendar and community centers are full. Putters try their swing in the Ice Golf Classic, played on packed snow. There are pool games and reindeer potlucks, poetry readings, spaghetti feeds, and a snowshoe softball tournament.

No matter what time of day or night, whether snow or rain is spitting from the sky, fans line the edges of Front Street to clap and cheer each musher and team into Nome. Some mushers collapse to the ground in exhaustion after crossing the finish line; others spend time answering questions from the media. Often, mushers have mixed feelings about

reaching the end. DeeDee Jonrowe, in her book *Iditarod Dreams* (1995), says of her 1994 race, a year when warm weather forced her to drop half her team, "On the morning after I finished, when I woke up in Nome, I... realized there was nothing more I could do. It was over.... No more miles to make up distance.... I really felt the post-race letdown." Even though she'd placed ninth out of 50, she nevertheless struggled with her own expectations, something every musher deals with when participating in a race of such length and repute. The 1991 Red Lantern Award recipient, Fairbanks's Brian O'Donoghue, says in his 1996 book

My Lead Dog Was a Lesbian, "From the instant I touched the arch, I began falling apart. The sun's glint on the snowy street seemed overly bright. Surrounding voices merged into a locker-room din. I felt that hot glow of staying awake all night, utterly drained, yet too excited to slow down." Many mushers tell of having dreams for several nights after they finish the Iditarod of someone urgently ordering them to get back on the trail and keep racing.

In Alaska's early days, when men drove dogs between roadhouses, a lantern was hung outside to help mushers find their way to shelter. Now, when the last musher in the Iditarod Trail Sled Dog Race reaches Nome, officials extinguish the "widow's lamp," a burning beacon hanging from the arch since 10 a.m. the day the race began. And each spring, even after the snow melts into the land, taking all the human and dog and sled tracks with it, the Iditarod Trail remains a solid historical and cultural presence. ◼

Managing the Trail

By Penny Rennick

Bureau of Land Management law enforcement rangers Dave Stimson, left, and Rohn Nelson take a break at Old Woman cabin, about 58 miles west of Kaltag. With about 1,500 residents spread along the sections of trail the men patrol, plus mushers and visitors following the race by snow machine or small plane, policing the trail has become a necessity. (Courtesy of Dave Stimson)

So who's in charge of the Iditarod Trail, during the sled dog race and the rest of the year? The short answer is the Bureau of Land Management (BLM), but just how this oversight works is a bit complicated. The Iditarod National Historic Trail is the only congressionally designated trail in Alaska, and the only such trail in the country that BLM manages. The trail itself crosses public and private land, with the bulk of the federal land being under BLM jurisdiction. The agency coordinates management through cooperative agreements and a comprehensive management plan among the various landowners. Having a single agency oversee the trail promotes consistency in policy and in what the public sees in relation to the trail. Regulations are uniform, signs are similar, allowed uses are coordinated. Mike Zaidlicz, Iditarod Trail coordinator for BLM, says that compared to other places, organizations representing the various users of the trail work well together, especially those that are part of the non-profit Iditarod National Historic Trail, Inc., which ensures that the trail is maintained for its recreational and historic value. This organization "is able to get its arms around the idea of the Iditarod."

Zaidlicz describes the Iditarod Trail as a "treasure, a jewel of traildom," and notes "that there are still people around who remember it and who used it" for travel and commerce during its heyday. In winter, "it was the major highway system for interior Alaska," he says. According to BLM, the main historical trail ran 938 miles from Seward to Nome, and had a total of 2,500 miles of trail segments. BLM rangers patrol the trail during permitted activities like the Iditarod sled dog race or the Iron Dog snow machine race. BLM staff also sweep the trail after events to ensure people are safe, cabins, bridges, and other infrastructure are intact and that needed maintenance is performed. For the sled dog race, BLM personnel concentrate between Rohn and

McGrath and between Kaltag and Unalakleet.

Policing the trail has allowed BLM personnel to collect vivid memories of the historical route. Dave Stimson, BLM district law enforcement ranger, recalls approaching Old Woman cabin in the dead silence of winter and seeing a bicycle on the porch, testimony to one of the Iditasport events. On another occasion, also along the portage, Stimson was passed by a snow machiner going "a hundred miles an hour." He found out later it was one of the Iron Dog racers on a training run. One morning when Zaidlicz was helping to build the new Old Woman cabin, he saw a 1,200-pound brown bear on its way to the coffee pot. Perhaps paramount among Zaidlicz's memories is the feeling of isolation on the trail. He says there are places where travelers can get a 360-degree view with no sign that anybody has ever been there. And he has had the opportunity to wander the Iditarod in summer, when much of the trail is underwater or otherwise inaccessible, something few others have been able to do.

As the overall coordinator for the trail, Zaidlicz has noted changes in the sled dog race in recent years. He says that sponsorships have changed. He thinks the race is now more controlled by local people and not as beholden to Outsiders as in the past. In his words, it is "now more of a local event and not so much a large corporate entity. It has an improved aura, more controlled by the participants, more fun and more self-supporting." Dave Stimson patrols the Kaltag to Unalakleet stretch where he reports that most of the local residents support the sled dog race because it puts a focus on their lives and brings in Outsiders and publicity. The Iron Dog, he says, "gets a mixed reception. Younger locals like it because they like the bigger, faster snow machines; older residents think it tears up the trail route." Stimson explains that in forested areas, snow machines tend to create moguls in the trail, which slow the mushers and can wreck their sleds. On the other hand, in open areas, the hard-packed trail

produced by frequent snow machine traffic can improve trail conditions for mushers and allow them to increase their speed and overall running time.

Intoxicated snow machine drivers have also kept BLM rangers busy. Although Unalakleet is a dry town, alcohol can be purchased at a liquor store along the Yukon River upstream from Kaltag. On the return trip to Unalakleet, snow machine drivers "under the influence" have jeopardized sled dog teams. For the 2001 race, Stimson and his partner, Rohn Nelson, let it be known in Unalakleet and Kaltag that they would be patrolling the portage. The instances of drunk driving were drastically reduced.

When asked what he hopes for the future of the Iditarod Trail, Mike Zaidlicz says he "would like a visitor or interpretive center at a historical site along the trail." Zaidlicz points out that enough people come to Alaska who are interested in the Iditarod races and the route that he thinks people would visit an interpretive center dedicated to the trail. □

Clearing the trail of debris such as fallen trees is another aspect of Dave Stimson's job during the Iditarod. Safety is the main goal. (Courtesy of Dave Stimson)

Checkpoints and Distances

By Susan Beeman

Mushers Ramy Brooks (in red vest), Doug Swingley, Bruce Moroney (background), Rick Swenson, and Martin Buser rest at Rohn. Brooks, who has been mushing since age four, is the son of sprint mushing champion Roxy Wright Champaine and grandson of Gareth Wright, a pioneer of modern sprint mushing. (Jeff Schultz/Alaska Stock)

EDITOR'S NOTE: *The 30th anniversary Iditarod Trail Sled Dog Race in 2002 will follow the northern route, which passes through 26 checkpoints, including Anchorage and Nome. In odd-numbered years, racers follow the southern route, with 27 stops. These alternate trails branch at Ophir and reconnect at Kaltag. Population figures for each checkpoint (from Alaska's Department of Community and Economic Development, 2000 census) are included in parentheses.*

Main Route

Mile 0: Anchorage (pop. 260,283) Excitement grips Alaska's largest city on the first Saturday in March. Thousands of spectators line Fourth Avenue and other city streets to watch teams race past on the first day of the Iditarod. The Millennium Hotel at the edge of Lake Hood houses the Race Operations Headquarters.

Mile 20: Eagle River (pop. 29,595) Saturday's run ends at the Eagle River VFW Post, where mushers remove their teams' harnesses and load the dogs into trucks. Mushers drive to Wasilla and prepare for Sunday's restart at 10 a.m.

Mile 49: Wasilla (pop. 5,469) Racers leave the restart chute in the same order as they did in Anchorage. Hundreds of spectators line the route snaking through Wasilla; snow machiners and other outdoor recreationists zip along the area's multitude of trails.

Mile 63: Knik (pop. 272) In the early 1900s, Knik was "outfitting central" for miners heading to the Iditarod area; today it's the Iditarod's last community on the connected road system. Mushers drop their tag sled and handler here and continue alone. Don Bowers, an Alaska musher who met an untimely death in the summer of 2000, kept a detailed account of the trail between 1996 and 1999; on the stretch between Knik and Yentna, he explained how snow machines affect the trail: "There will be ruts, bumps, rough spots, and moguls.... There will be hundreds of snow machiners [on the Susitna River] to cheer you on; it should be getting dark about this time and you can see their bonfires scattered for miles on up the river."

Mile 115: Yentna Station Roadhouse (pop. 8) Dan and Jean Gabryszak and their children live here year-round, opening their home and roadhouse to mushers during the Iditarod.

Mile 149: Skwentna (pop. 111) Bowers called this checkpoint a "beehive of activity," as most racers are still traveling bunched together and all arrive here the first evening. It's also home to Joe and Norma Delia, who open their two-story log house to mushers and visitors during every Iditarod. The trail beyond Skwentna crosses the Skwentna River where the old Skwentna Roadhouse, one of the original Iditarod Trail roadhouses, used to stand. About halfway between Skwentna and Finger Lake, "dozens and sometimes hundreds of people will fly their ski planes, run their snow machines, and drive their dog teams out to a huge bonfire blowout that starts on Sunday night and continues well into Monday," wrote Bowers. Many mushers, he said, stop for a few minutes of socializing and snacking.

Mile 194: Finger Lake (pop. 2) In recent years, a mobile espresso stand has been set up at this stop, continuing the tradition of grassroots commerce on the trail that dates back to the race's beginnings. In 1974 and 1975, Gene and June Leonard, the previous residents at Finger Lake, would relay to the Beeman family living at Farewell Lake via radio that the front runners were on their way; the Beemans would boil water for tea and cocoa and bake cookies for their trailside "teahouse," inviting mushers to stop for a few minutes and warm up. Gene ran the Iditarod four times, finishing twice. Today, Kristen and Carl Dixon live here and operate Winter Lake Lodge. Just past Finger Lake are what mushers call the "dreaded" Happy River steps, a series of steep descents to Happy River valley. "Notorious" Round Mountain also tests skills over a short, twisting, often icy section of trail.

Mile 224: Rainy Pass (pop. 2) Tucked into the Alaska Range, this checkpoint at elevation 1,835 feet is only a few miles from the highest point along the trail, 3,160 feet. Mushers sleep and eat inside two of Vern Humble's cabins at Puntilla Lake; the big game guide's hunting operation here is closed during winter. After leaving Rainy Pass, mushers enter the infamous Dalzell Gorge, which, according to Bowers, can be "nothing more than a very scenic exercise in

sled driving, or...your worst nightmare come true," depending on conditions. Snow, glare ice, and open water can send teams, mushers, and sleds tumbling.

Mile 272: Rohn (pop. 0) Rohn Roadhouse marks the transition between the Alaska Range and the flat Interior; temperatures usually drop accordingly. Many mushers take their 24-hour layover here, site of the original roadhouse used by mail carriers in the early twentieth century; the checkpoint's cabin was built in the 1930s. Lack of visitor facilities makes this a quiet place to rest the dogs.

Mile 352: Nikolai (pop. 100) This is another favorite place for the long layover, especially after crossing the Farewell Burn, and is the first of several Native villages along the route. A trading post and roadhouse were among Nikolai's businesses during the gold rush in the early twentieth century; the town's present site was established in 1918.

Central Yup'ik musher Mike Williams of Akiak, a small village near the mouth of the Kuskokwim River, stirs dog food in Nikolai. Known as the "sobriety musher" for his support of Native sobriety, Williams spends time in Alaska communities when not on the runners of a dog sled, giving motivational speeches. He has twice received Providence Alaska Medical Center's Most Inspirational Musher Award for his leadership on the Iditarod Trail. (Jeff Schultz/Alaska Stock)

RIGHT: *For lack of structurally sound buildings at the ghost town of Iditarod, a "Dodge Lodge" is set up as the official checkpoint. After Jim Lanier stops his team, made up of all white dogs bred at his kennel specifically for that trait, he will present his veterinarian notebook to be marked off as a vet inspects each dog. (Jeff Schultz/Alaska Stock)*

LOWER RIGHT: *In even years teams follow a northern route between Ophir and Kaltag. Sixty miles northeast of Ophir, Jeff King spreads straw for his dogs to lie on at Cripple. By the time Walter L. Goodwin made his second reconnaissance of the trail in 1910, Cripple had become the mining region's largest service station in terms of manpower, supplies, and mail. Today, the old town stands silent except during the Iditarod. (Loren Taft)*

Mile 400: McGrath (pop. 354) The first musher into McGrath receives PenAir's Spirit of Alaska Award, reflecting the musher's perseverance. The Iditarod Trail, heavily used between 1911 and 1920, went through McGrath; by 1907, the town, named after Peter McGrath, a local U.S. Marshal, had taken hold and grown into a regional supply center for Innoko District miners. In 1909, Alaska Commercial Company opened a store. The Federal Aviation Administration built a communications complex here in 1940; McGrath became an important fueling stop during WWII, as part of the Lend-Lease Program between the United States and Russia.

Mile 418: Takotna (pop. 50) Another favorite for the 24-hour layover, Takotna offers racers lots of homemade food any time of day or night and a "mushers-only" church for peaceful napping.

Mile 443: Ophir (pop. 0) Named by Elias Honaen, a prospector, in 1908 for the lost country of Ophir, the source of King Solomon's gold, this ghost town checkpoint was hosted by Dick and Audra Forsgren, who own a cabin nearby, for many years. They've since passed on the honor to their son, Keith.

ALTERNATE ROUTE, EVEN YEARS

Mile 503: Cripple (pop. 0) The first musher to this halfway point along the northern route gets the GCI Dorothy G. Page Halfway Award: a trophy and $3,000 in gold nuggets, symbolic of the area's mining history.

LEFT, TOP: *Winter temperatures at Shageluk range from minus 60 degrees Fahrenheit to zero and annual snowfall averages nine feet, but Iditarod mushers get a warm welcome from residents. (Jeff Schultz/ Alaska Stock)*

LEFT, BOTTOM: *Jack Berry from Fritz Creek, near Homer, pulls into Galena along the Yukon River in 1998, echoing Edgar Nollner's arrival in 1925 carrying the package of diphtheria serum for Nome residents. Athabaskans had seasonal subsistence camps in the Galena area before a supply camp formed for prospectors working nearby galena mines. The Natives began moving to Galena in 1920 to sell wood to steamboats; when the original townsite flooded, the community moved to its current location on the north bank of the Yukon. (Jeff Schultz/Alaska Stock)*

Charlie Boulding and his team pull into Kaltag, on the Yukon River. Kaltag was established soon after a measles epidemic and food shortage in 1900 killed one-third of the area's Athabaskan population; survivors of three other villages regrouped there. Kaltag is the last Iditarod checkpoint on the notoriously windy river. (Fred Hirschmann)

Mile 615: Ruby (pop. 188) After the 112-mile stretch between Cripple and Ruby, mushers are glad to rest at the first checkpoint on the Yukon River, an Athabaskan community and home to Iditarod champion Emmitt Peters. The Millennium Hotel's First Musher to the Yukon Award is presented here as a seven-course dinner and $3,500 in cash.

Mile 667: Galena (pop. 675) Snow machine travel on the Yukon River is heavy from Galena to Nulato and Kaltag, and mushers share the frozen waterway with residents checking traplines, hunting, or hauling freight and passengers between villages.

Mile 719: Nulato (pop. 336) Nulato's community hall serves as the checkpoint, belying the village's violent history; Natives burned down Russian trading posts established in 1838 and 1841. Today's

site was built in 1853. The northern route meets the main Iditarod Trail again in Kaltag.

ALTERNATE ROUTE, ODD YEARS

Mile 533: Iditarod (pop. 0) The next checkpoint after Ophir during odd-year races is the ghost town for which the Iditarod National Historic Trail was named and is the halfway point. The ITC provides a heated shelter here and awards the first musher to arrive the GCI Dorothy G. Page Award. Teams face hilly terrain between Iditarod and Shageluk.

Mile 598: Shageluk (pop. 129) The name of the town means "village of the dog people," an appropriate description for an Iditarod checkpoint.

Mile 623: Anvik (pop. 104) A church bell rings for the first musher entering Anvik, signaling residents that the winner of the seven-course meal and cash prize for beating fellow racers to the Yukon River has arrived.

Mile 641: Grayling (pop. 194) Like other Interior communities, Grayling temperatures can plummet to minus 60 degrees Fahrenheit; prevailing north winds along the Yukon River add an extra challenge to mushing in subzero conditions.

Mile 701: Eagle Island (pop. 1) Other than Ralph Conaster, an Eagle Island resident for many years, this checkpoint is deserted but still a welcome respite from the monotony of driving dogs around bend after bend of the Yukon River. Teams pass sloughs and bluffs and often have to help push the sled over windblown, sandy trail before reaching Kaltag.

Main Route

(Mileage shown is for even years; total odd-year distance is 10 miles longer.)

Mile 761: Kaltag (pop. 230) Wind and snow can cover the trail in minutes along the Yukon River; Kaltag provides a break from harsh weather as the trail from here crosses Kaltag Portage toward the Norton Sound coast and its own brand of wind. In good conditions, the run from Kaltag to Unalakleet takes 10 to 15 hours, longer in a storm. Mushers can stop at the Tripod Flats cabin, 35 miles west of Kaltag or at the Old Woman cabin, several miles farther west; BLM manages both. Iditarod veterans advise visitors passing through to leave an offering of food for the "Old Woman" so her ghost won't follow them down the trail.

Mile 851: Unalakleet (pop. 747) The first musher into Unalakleet, an Inupiaq word meaning "place where the east wind blows," receives the Wells Fargo Gold Coast Award: a trophy and $2,500 worth of gold nuggets. This is the largest community on the Iditarod Trail between Wasilla and Nome.

Mile 893: Shaktoolik (pop. 230) Snowdrifts around this village testify to the constant wind. Mushers leave here and enter the most exposed section of the entire trail that leads across Norton Bay, an area notorious for storms. Bowers called it "bleak, flat, and deadly monotonous." Lead dogs sometimes balk at the white expanse and refuse to budge.

Mile 941: Koyuk (pop. 297) Mushers consider Koyuk a refuge from the icy, whiteout conditions of the Norton Bay crossing.

Mile 989: Elim (pop. 313) Racers begin to "sprint" from here, only 123 miles from the finish line.

Mile 1,017: Golovin (pop. 144) Most mushers stop only long enough at Golovin to check in, check out, then continue as they try to catch up to and pass the teams ahead of them.

Mile 1,035: White Mountain (pop. 203) All mushers must take an eight-hour rest here before donning their finisher's bib and proceeding. This town grew after an influx of gold seekers arrived in Nome in 1900; miner Charles Lane built the first structure, a warehouse, to store supplies for his nearby claim.

Mile 1,090: Safety (pop. 0) Mushers jettison unnecessary gear and race to the finish line, only 22 miles away. Relinquishing the trail to another racer is not mandatory in "no man's land," the last three miles of trail into Nome.

Mile 1,112: Nome (pop. 3,505) Passing under the burled arch, each team gets a spirited welcome. The long journey is finished. □

LEFT: *Inupiaq children in Elim, 123 miles from the finish line, greet dogs in Matt Desalernos's team. Desalernos, who has run the Iditarod 10 times and placed seventh in 1993, lives in Nome. (Barb Willard)*

BELOW: *On a bank of the Unalakleet River between Kaltag and the Norton Sound coast, Rick Mackey hops off the runners to help push his sled uphill at mile 693 of the historic Iditarod route, beginning in Seward. The Unalakleet checkpoint is the last refuge for mushers before they head out along the edge of the sea ice. (Jeff Schultz/Alaska Stock)*

Iditarod Hall of Fame

Jerry Austin, age 54
Home: St. Michael, AK

1976	23rd
1978	9th
1980	7th
1981	13th
1982	3rd
1984	5th
1985	14th
1986	8th
1987	5th
1988	11th
1989	22nd
1990	19th
1991	14th
1992	24th
1993	23rd
1994	22nd
1995	17th
1996	21st

Checkers at Nikolai show Jerry Austin where he can park his team on a frosty morning. The best part of running the Iditarod, says the musher, is "just being out on the trail with your friends." (Jeff Schultz/ Alaska Stock)

By Susan Beeman

EDITOR'S NOTE: *In 1997, the* Anchorage Daily News *established the Iditarod Hall of Fame to honor people whose contributions have distinguished the Iditarod Trail Sled Dog Race. Every year, a committee of race-savvy journalists chooses finalists from nominations offered by race experts and other knowledgeable* Daily News *staff. The list spotlights the accomplishments of mushers, veterinarians, trailbreakers, and others who've supported the race in a variety of ways. So far, 12 mushers, one trailbreaker/checker, and one veterinarian have been inducted into the Hall. There were no inductees in 2000.*

Inducted in 1997

As a three-time winner of the Sportsmanship Award, **Jerry Austin** of St. Michael, a primarily Central Yup'ik village of 368 on Norton Sound, has earned respect and appreciation from other mushers, from doing the smallest favors to helping save fellow contestant Mike Madden's life in 1989 after Madden became sick and delusional on the trail.

Austin, who moved to Alaska from Seattle, began assembling a dog team after listening to reports of the first Iditarod race on the radio. Carl Huntington, the 1974 winner, gave four of his championship dogs to Austin. A commercial fisherman, lodge owner, and bush pilot, Austin already knew how to look after himself in the woods, and he quickly adapted to the rigors of dog mushing. He entered the Iditarod nearly every year between 1976 and 1996.

One year, Austin says, the townspeople of Elim, a checkpoint east of Nome, had tacked signs to several buildings warning of polar bear sightings, unusual so far south. Another time, in 1985, as his team sped around a notoriously icy corner on the trail past Finger Lake, Austin's sled crashed into a tree and he broke his hand. Thirty miles farther, at Rainy Pass, fellow musher and doctor Jacques Philip fashioned a cast from a coat hanger and tape, which Austin says lasted until he reached the Yukon River. There, his hand came dangerously close to freezing, wrapped in the cast inside his mitten.

"So I chewed the cast off," he says. It was too cold to remove his other hand from his mitten.

None of these setbacks stopped him from returning to race each year, but the desire to spend time with his son, Tony, did. Hunting and fishing now keep the pair busy through every season as they set out on week-long camping trips with teams from their 55-dog lot.

"I'd like to run the race again," Austin says. "Maybe when my son gets out of college."

Now, each year after the race at the awards ceremony in Nome, Austin and his wife, Clara, present the Rookie of the Year Award to the top-finishing rookie. The $1,500 comes from the Austins' pockets.

From fierce coastal storms to hallucinations to a moose attack that killed two and injured 13 of her dogs, **Susan Butcher** has faced all manner of challenges on the Iditarod Trail. This race veteran who sings to her dogs between checkpoints has won the race four times, garnering national media attention, but nowhere is she more popular than here in Alaska. Among the mushing community, she's respected for her hard work, fairness, honesty, and spunk, and for taking exceptional care of her dogs. In fact, they are some of her best friends, and regularly join her and husband Dave Monson, also an Iditarod musher, inside the couple's cabin in Fairbanks, for socializing and play. Butcher is a favorite in the general public's eye, too, especially as a role model for other female athletes — she was the first woman to finish the Iditarod in the top 20, the top 10, and the top five. Three of her victories followed one after the other, in 1986, 1987, and 1988, making Butcher the first musher to achieve the grand prize three times straight. She won again in 1990. Training with Redington in previous years and living alone in Alaska's Wrangell Mountains had paid off.

After the 1994 race, her last time as a contestant, Butcher decided it was time to start a family. She chose her first child's middle name to commemorate one of her favorite lead dogs, Tekla. While spending much of her time as a parent, Butcher has still found time for the Iditarod by reporting from the trail during the race. "I was born with the pioneering spirit," she says.

Dick Mackey won the Iditarod by the closest margin ever in 1978 when his lead dogs Skipper and Shrew crossed the finish line one second ahead of Rick Swenson's, firmly establishing the convention that the first dog nose across the line, not the musher or sled, determines the official time of arrival in

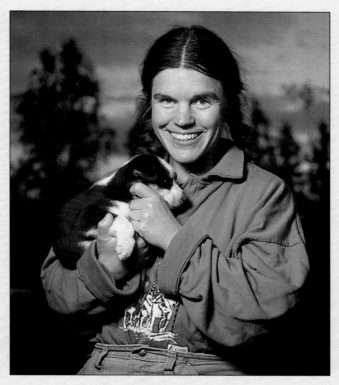

Susan Butcher cradles a possible future Iditarod leader. Butcher last ran the Iditarod in 1994, after which she announced her retirement from the race to raise a family with her husband Dave Monson, also an Iditarod veteran. (Jeff Schultz/Alaska Stock)

Nome. Mackey consistently finished in the top 10 in his first six Iditarods, and has been a tireless advocate and organizer for the race. His dedication to the mushers, dogs, and spirit of the Iditarod haven't waned since the last time he ran the race, in 1987.

His sons, Bill, Rick (1983 Iditarod champion), Lance, and Jason have benefitted from their father's experience on the trail. "When Rick won," says Mackey, "there was lots more to see. You're watching it unfold." Of his own experience claiming victory, he points out that "you're just doing it, and the next day you say, 'Oh, I won.'"

Spurred by Jack London adventure stories, Mackey came to Alaska from New Hampshire in 1958. This veteran musher helped Redington clear the old Iditarod Trail on foot with chainsaws between Old

Susan Butcher, age 47
Home: Fairbanks, AK

1978	19th
1979	9th
1980	5th
1981	5th
1982	2nd
1983	9th
1984	2nd
1985	Scratched
1986	1st
1987	1st
1988	1st
1989	2nd
1990	1st
1991	3rd
1992	2nd
1993	4th
1994	10th

Dick Mackey, age 69
Home: Nenana, AK

1973	7th
1974	10th
1975	7th
1976	8th
1977	6th
1978	1st
1980	Scratched
1987	32nd

Herbie Nayokpuk, age 72
Home: Shishmaref, AK

1973	5th
1974	3rd
1975	4th
1979	Scratched
1980	2nd
1981	7th
1982	12th
1983	4th
1985	8th
1987	25th
1988	6th

Emmitt Peters, age 61
Home: Ruby, AK

1975	1st
1976	5th
1977	4th
1978	3rd
1979	2nd
1980	9th
1981	12th
1982	4th
1983	19th
1984	17th
1985	12th
1990	41st
1992	Scratched
2000	40th

RIGHT: *Skipper led Dick Mackey's team to victory in the 1978 Iditarod. At 45, Mackey was then the oldest winner. (Bill Devine)*

FAR RIGHT: *Emmitt Peters steals a nap on his sled at Skwentna in 1985, his 11th Iditarod. His advice for rookies? "Train, train, train, and take good care of your dogs." (Jeff Schultz/Alaska Stock)*

Skwentna Roadhouse and Susitna Station for the 1967 Centennial race. He was president of the ITC one year, and has provided live TV commentary and emceed Iditarod banquets.

The most dangerous section of trail, Mackey remembers, was near Hellsgate on the South Fork of the Kuskokwim River in Ptarmigan Valley, the route taken for the first few years of the race between Finger Lake and Rohn. There was "lots of overflow, lots of holes," he says. "It was a violent piece of river."

Mackey and his wife are enjoying retirement and spend a few months each year in Arizona. He still follows the Iditarod race and is a judge at others.

Herbie Nayokpuk, nicknamed "The Shishmaref Cannonball" after his hometown on northwestern Seward Peninsula and his speedy second-place arrival at Nome's finish line in 1980, remains legendary in the eyes of fellow mushers and Iditarod fans. Competing in the first three Iditarod races and in

several others throughout the 1980s, Nayokpuk earned a reputation as being both kind and tough. He gives his reason for entering his first Iditarod as, "because I was always mushing anyway."

In 1983, at the age of 53, he finished fourth despite having undergone open-heart surgery five months before the race. Race organizers in 1992 bestowed honorary bib number one, traditionally given each year in salute to a musher or non-musher who's made a significant contribution to dog-racing and the Iditarod, to Nayokpuk, the first living musher to receive it.

Nayokpuk and Joe Redington often mushed or sat out storms together along the Iditarod Trail, and they traveled to Washington D.C. with Col. Norman Vaughan to partake in the parade celebrating President Ronald Reagan's 1981 inauguration. Nayokpuk referred to their group as "The Three Stooges."

He's now retired from dog racing but continues to be an enthusiastic supporter of old-time mushers and newcomers to the Iditarod Trail Sled Dog Race.

Athabaskan musher **Emmitt Peters** is one of only three rookies to have won the Iditarod (the others are Dick Wilmarth, 1973, and Carl Huntington, 1974). Peters grew up in Ruby, the first Yukon River check-

Emmitt H. Peters Jr. ↑ *Alice Ranger*

Best wishes
6/10/02
future Iditarod
musher
There's my dad!
Grandpa Ruby Longcreek Mine

point on the northern route, surrounded by his family's working dogs. When he pulled ahead of the front runners in the 1975 race to cross the finish line in 14 days, 14 hours, and 43 minutes, the crowd on Nome's Front Street went wild at news of the new Iditarod record — six days faster than either previous winner. Peters's system of giving his team short rest periods on the trail, rather than running all day and camping all night, had paid off; he was named Rookie of the Year.

"My mother didn't understand this 24-hour layover," which he took in Ruby, says Peters. She "kept waking me up every couple of hours, saying 'they're leaving, they're leaving.'" Peters felt drowsy the next day and napped in his sled as his dogs pulled him. He passed two other teams while dozing.

Peters remembers being disoriented as a rookie when he reached the Norton Sound coast. "I was used to the timber of inland, but out there, it was miles and miles of nothing. Running at night was like you're running out in space."

Hallucinations are a fact on the Iditarod Trail from lack of sleep, and Peters says he once thought he saw a snow machine coming straight toward him, so he stopped his team and walked up to it and said hello. "It was a chunk of ice," he laughs. Another hallucination presented him with what he thought was a low tree. "I ducked and hit my chin on the handle bars. It woke me up."

Dubbed "The Yukon Fox" for his speed and strategy, Peters remained in the top-10 finishers for the next five years. A knee injury kept him out of the race in the late 1980s, but he returned to the line-up three more times. Though he never caught up to the new front-runners, he received the Most Inspirational Musher Award in 2000, and now volunteers as a checker in his home village.

Without **Joe Redington Sr.**, there would be no sled dog race from Anchorage to Nome; it was, after all, his idea. Redington, who died in 1999 at 82, never did

In exchange for advertising on his truck, sled, and clothing, sponsors supported Joe Redington's many years on the Iditarod Trail. During the race, many mushers wear a coat or hat with a sponsor's logo sewn on, such as Redington does here in his blue parka. (Barb Willard)

win the race he worked so hard to create and nurture, but that didn't bother him.

"He would have liked to win," says his wife, Vi, "but he just loved that race and the trail. He worked hard to get the trail saved as a National Historic Trail."

Redington's talents lay in his enthusiasm for the sport, his support of younger mushers, and his dedication to family and friends. Redington and trail-breaker Joe Delia of Skwentna helped navigate the first section of trail before the inaugural race. Delia's snow machine broke down, and he remembers Redington landing his plane "in a [frozen] swamp" to see if he could help. Three times Redington received awards for being the Iditarod's most inspirational contender. With his wife and children, Redington started Knik Kennels in 1948, and by 1990 more than 500 dogs lived on the lot. He leased up to 10 teams at a time to beginners; many of those dogs became members of other mushers' Iditarod teams.

Longtime friend Bill Devine of Anchorage says, "Everybody liked the guy 'cause he fought back," against critics of the Iditarod and those who at first told him it couldn't be done.

Says Vi, "He liked competition, but he loved mushing." He knew how important fans of the race

Joe Redington Sr.,
died 1999, age 82
Home: Knik, AK

1974	11th
1975	5th
1976	Scratched
1977	5th
1978	5th
1979	10th
1980	Scratched
1981	14th
1982	17th
1984	7th
1985	Scratched
1986	Scratched
1987	33rd
1988	5th
1989	9th
1990	25th
1991	31st
1992	41st
1997	36th

Libby Riddles, age 45
Home: Homer, AK

1980	18th
1981	20th
1985	1st
1987	Scratched
1989	16th
1995	32nd

Rick Swenson, age 51
Home: Two Rivers, AK

1976	10th
1977	1st
1978	2nd
1979	1st
1980	4th
1981	1st
1982	1st
1983	5th
1984	6th
1985	4th
1986	3rd
1987	2nd
1988	2nd
1989	3rd
1990	7th
1991	1st
1992	4th
1993	9th
1994	4th
1995	10th
1996	Withdrawn
1998	11th
1999	4th
2000	8th
2001	4th

were too. Of the last stretch of trail during his first Iditarod, in 1974, Redington told Dorothy Page, "By the time I got close to Nome…at least 75 kids were trailing behind me, begging for a ride. I gave about 25 of them a ride. They sure loved that."

Joe Redington Sr. was buried, as he'd requested, in a dogsled.

News of **Libby Riddles**'s unprecedented victory in 1985 flew around the nation as fast as the media could transmit the story. She was the first woman to win the Iditarod in its 13-year history.

"It was very bizarre," she says of the instant fame. "I took it with such a sense of humor, but it was a real thrill. They told me I had the biggest [newspaper] headline since statehood." Suddenly, national magazines were publishing articles and photo essays about Riddles, then 28, who lived in Teller, 60 miles north of Nome. All the residents in Teller were pulling for her, including Iditarod mushing partner Joe Garnie, who loaned her several dogs for her winning team that year.

"People would call and want a picture of me in a dress in the dog yard," she laughs now, remembering all the attention. Requests for speaking engagements and invitations to television studios outside Alaska flooded her answering machine and mailbox, and she recalls meeting Bill Cosby and having "donuts with him before some show."

Sixteen years later, the fawning has faded, but her reputation as a top-notch musher has not. Riddles spent the summer of 2001 in Juneau giving lectures about dog mushing and running the Iditarod, focusing on the variety of people who run the race.

"I also like to play up the fun times on the trail," she explains, "since the race is always portrayed as so grueling."

Riddles did face a grueling push to the finish line in 1985. In Nome, her leaders Dugan and Axle received the Lolly Medley Memorial Golden Harness Award for leading the team through that year's

infamous Norton Sound storm that kept other mushers bundled in their sleeping bags at the Shaktoolik checkpoint. She emphasizes how proud she was of her dogs.

With the help of Tim Jones, author of *The Last Great Race* (1982), Riddles told of her adventures in a book called *Race Across Alaska: First woman to win the Iditarod tells her story* (1988); several years later she wrote a children's book, illustrated by Alaska artist Shannon Cartwright, called *Storm Run* (1996).

When asked if she plans to run the Iditarod again, she chuckles and says, "I'm kinda trying to quit." She's in the midst of a different adventure now — building a house in Homer, 226 road miles southwest of Anchorage. She'll keep her dogs in racing shape, though, training in the nearby Caribou Hills.

Rick Swenson has proven five times that he and his team can go the distance faster than any others. His Iditarod race credits also include top-10 placement in 23 out of 25 races. Winning, though, isn't a prerequisite for a Hall of Fame nomination. Swenson has also received other Iditarod awards for sportsmanship, being the first competitor to reach the Yukon River, taking exceptional care of his team throughout the race, and having outstanding lead dogs.

Originally from the Boundary Waters area of Minnesota, Swenson grew up near a trapper and grilled the man about outdoor living skills; he started mushing because he wanted the freedom to travel through wilderness. He read about the first Iditarod when he was 22, moved to Alaska the next year, and bought a few sled dogs from Joe Redington. Throughout the next few years, trapping and bush living in winter and working on the trans-Alaska oil pipeline in summer occupied Swenson.

He now makes his home in Two Rivers, about 30 miles east of Fairbanks. The first time he won the Iditarod, 1977, Swenson used a sled he'd built himself, by hand.

As a 52-year resident of Skwentna, **Joe Delia** knows the Iditarod Trail. He officially broke trail with his snow machine during the first few years of the race, from Skwentna 40 miles southeast to the Susitna River and 45 miles northwest to Finger Lake. Volunteering as checker in his hometown from 1978 to 1981 and from 1983 to 1997, Delia and his wife, Norma, opened their two-story cabin to mushers, fans, and other volunteers every March.

Since 1949, Delia has been trapping in the area; his line ran northwest of the old Mountain Climber's Roadhouse in 1972 when Redington enlisted his help in surveying the old Iditarod Trail for the upcoming race. The men found it impassable by overgrown brush and alders, but the U.S. Army aided them by combining cold-weather practice maneuvers with marking the race route. Delia remembers checking his trap line only to find "survey markers on his marten sets." The Army was supposed to have cleared the historical trail, but instead followed one already open.

Delia had a small dog team for several years, which he used to check his trap line and haul freight. "With a small team and the heavy snows of this country, the dog driver is the biggest dog in the team. Lots of snowshoeing ahead breaking trail," he muses. He never seriously considered running the Iditarod. "I wouldn't put myself in the hole financially," he says, citing the cost of preparing for and running the race today. "But right after I got rid of my team," he says, "my daughter got 22 dogs." Christine (Delia) Kriger, now retired from mushing, won the Jr. Iditarod in 1981, the only girl to claim victory.

In 1982, Delia served as Iditarod race judge, the eyes and ears of the race marshal, keeping "a journal of just about anything that happened along the trail with comments and suggestions." He got to visit many villages, and has met hundreds of people as checkpoint host, some becoming close friends. Though he's never run the Iditarod with a dog team, Delia's presence along the trail is undeniable.

Joe Delia, right, has played many roles along the Iditarod Trail, including trailbreaker, checker, race judge, and all-around hospitable Alaskan. In this 1975 photo, he stops for coffee with fellow trailbreaker Frank Harvey of Wasilla between Rohn and Farewell Lake. (Marydith Beeman)

Bob Sept first took an interest in the Iditarod Trail Sled Dog Race when he moved to Alaska in 1979. He's never run the race himself, but as chief Iditarod veterinarian in 1981 and 1982, he spent hundreds of hours free of charge inspecting dogs, and in general, raising the race's standards for dog care. As race president from 1983 to 1985, Sept helped keep the financially ailing ITC's head above water.

"It was a year to year deal," he says of race financing. "We had a mountain to climb. We had to get new sponsors."

In 1983, the organization was $100,000 in debt, but once they incorporated new promotional tactics, including merchandise, collectibles, and raffle tickets, new sources of income appeared. Another turning point for the Iditarod came, he explains, when Libby Riddles won in 1985, making the name "Iditarod" a household word and convincing sponsors to invest more money.

Knowledge of canine health, says Sept, has improved dramatically since the race's early years. Beginning in 1980, at his request, Cornell University, site of a toxicology program "on the cutting edge" of testing the front-runners in horse racing, began drug

Joe Delia, age 72
Home: Skwentna, AK

1973-1977 ... Trailbreaker and handyman
1978-1981 and 1983-1997.....
    Skwentna checkpoint checker
1982 .... Race judge

Bob Sept, age 54
Home: Chugiak, AK

1981 and 1982 ....Chief veterinarian
1983-1985 .... Race president
2000 Golden Stethoscope Award
Currently... veterinarian, checker, rules committee member

Martin Buser, age 43
Home: Big Lake, AK

1980	22nd
1981	19th
1986	25th
1987	10th
1988	3rd
1989	6th
1990	10th
1991	2nd
1992	1st
1993	6th
1994	1st
1995	2nd
1996	3rd
1997	1st
1998	8th
1999	2nd
2000	7th
2001	24th

As one of 30 to 35 official Iditarod veterinarians, Bob Sept of Chugiak knows how to keep long-distance dogs healthy; here he inspects a member of Shaktoolik musher Palmer Sagoonick's team. Comparing today's race to the early years, Sept says there is no longer "all the commiserating and camaraderie now, no big bonfires along the trail between checkpoints," but he does think the dogs are still "tremendous athletes." (Jeff Schultz/Alaska Stock)

testing Iditarod dogs, a practice that continues to be refined. Informed feeding practices were lacking during the 1973 race, Sept notes, recalling that mushers fed their dogs primarily high protein commercial kibble, which didn't include enough fat to keep them strong when running long distances. Some mushers bought beaver from trappers along the trail to supplement dry food.

"Those dogs burn 6,000 to 8,000 calories a day," during the Iditarod says Sept, with some consuming even more. Today's veterinarians have a much clearer idea of how to keep long-distance sled dogs healthy.

Sept's favorite place to spend time on the Iditarod Trail is the Rohn checkpoint. He's drawn to its location, "right in the heart of the Alaska Range... with mountains all around and not a lot of people."

Inducted in 1998

Big Lake musher **Martin Buser**, originally from Switzerland, has run the Iditarod the past 16 years in a row. He came to Alaska in 1979, worked as a dog handler for sprint musher Earl Norris in Willow, and ran his first Iditarod in 1980, placing 22nd; the next year he moved up to 19th. Alaska's open spaces convinced him to make the state his home; he now owns Happy Trails Kennel, home to 79 dogs and several handlers, some of whom have trained with Buser to emerge as Iditarod mushers themselves.

"We get different handlers every year," Buser explains. "Most of them come up to learn about sled dogs." His 2001 handler, Kurt Dally, from Washington, plans to participate in the 2002 Serum Run.

A vigilant trainer, Buser pays attention to each of his dog's quirks, matching athletes by personality, size, and gait. Once he's on the Iditarod Trail, when his team is running well, Buser takes what he calls a "mental-health minute," in which he stops and anchors the sled and moves through the team dog by dog, petting and praising each one. By the time he's done, they're all barking and lunging, ready again to run. This positive reinforcement approach to dog training and care, though, is not unique.

"It's a trend in animal husbandry — ignore the negative and reward the positive," he says. "You just achieve better results that way."

Buser and his wife, Kathy Chapoton, named their sons after Iditarod checkpoints Nikolai and Rohn. Buser says Nikolai, 13, is starting to get interested in mushing and talks about running the Jr. Iditarod.

"I'm trying not to let him get too 'doggy,'" Buser says, "because with all the fun comes all the responsibility."

That responsibility comes in many forms, from sponsorship obligations to deciding which dogs to include in a particular race. In the 2001 Iditarod, Buser had to drop three dogs early in the race. Falling behind, he struggled over ice, bare ground, and exposed rocks between Finger Lake and Takotna, bruising his confidence as much as his body and sled. Slush and headwinds slowed the team even more, prompting Buser to dub his 18th Iditarod a "disaster."

"I guess every 18 years I can put up with [a bad race]," he concedes, but prefers instead to look forward. His 2002 Iditarod team is shaping up well. "I'm looking forward to improving on last year's race."

Inducted in 1999

Among the Iditarod's multiple winners is **Jeff King** of Denali Park. In 1975, he moved to Alaska from California and entered his first sled dog race, placing third. A successful competitor from the outset of his mushing career, King's determination has led him to three Iditarod championships in the 1990s and victories in the Yukon Quest (1989), Kuskokwim 300, and International Stage Stop Sled Dog Race that covers nearly 500 miles of Wyoming's backcountry.

He's come a long way to the winner's circle from where he began in the mid 1970s, sitting in his wilderness cabin listening to a static-marred radio broadcast of one of the first Iditarod races, a husky pup on his lap. King keeps more than 80 dogs in shape during the summer by letting them loose to swim after him as he paddles his canoe around Goose Lake, for which he named his kennel. Two or three handlers help him train teams; usually one handler plans specifically to race a young team in the Iditarod, giving both dogs and handler invaluable experience.

"It's also a kind of compensation for [the handlers] in exchange for their hard work," says King.

About his own dedication he explains, "The Iditarod focuses so many of my interests into one place. It's an annual goal." And though he thinks the intense competition doesn't always bring out the best in people, his love of mushing sustains his desire to keep racing. Images of the trail also inspire him. One night a couple of years ago, "a sliver of moon, a

Taking a break at Takotna's town hall, Jeff King calls home to give his family an update on his progress. The 18 miles separating McGrath and Takotna are his favorite, he says, because of the wilderness scenery. (Jeff Schultz/Alaska Stock)

brilliant dark blue sky, and the aurora" accompanied him as he left the Ruby checkpoint.

Inducted in 2001

Don Bowers was a teacher, bush pilot, United States Air Force pilot, volunteer in the Iditarod Air Force, and musher. He was killed in a plane crash near Denali in 2000, but lives on in the hearts of family and friends and as a member of the Iditarod Hall of Fame. Don finished three out of the five races he entered from 1995 to 1999. He never had visions of winning, but an adventurous streak ran deep in this Arkansan turned Alaskan. Besides mushing the trail, he wrote books on flying, compiled an Iditarod Trail guide, and published *Back of the Pack: An Iditarod Rookie Musher's Alaska Pilgrimage to Nome* (1998), a book that details his love for the Iditarod, his training schedule the year before his first attempt, his disappointing first try, and finally an account of his successful finish.

As an Iditarod Air Force pilot ferrying reporters, photographers, mushers who'd scratched, dropped dogs, and gear and witnessing joy and anguish along the trail, Bowers asked himself, "Who are these

Jeff King, age 46
Home: Denali Park, AK

1981	28th
1991	12th
1992	6th
1993	1st
1994	3rd
1995	7th
1996	1st
1997	3rd
1998	1st
1999	7th
2000	3rd
2001	3rd

Don Bowers, died 2000, age 52
Home: Willow, AK

1995	Scratched
1996	48th
1997	40th
1998	Scratched
1999	44th

RIGHT: *Don Bowers shares a laugh during the 1997 Iditarod. Never a contender for the top 10 or even the top 20, he considered the race a personal challenge and a fun, exciting way to spend time with his team. Bowers died in 2000. (Jeff Schultz/Alaska Stock)*

FAR RIGHT: *Four-time winner and current champion Doug Swingley attributes his mushing success to having well-bred dogs conditioned to keep a steady pace over long distances. The Montana musher's 2000 victory was the fastest time from Anchorage to Nome in the race's history. (Jeff Schultz/Alaska Stock)*

Doug Swingley, age 48
Home: Lincoln, MT

1992	9th
1993	8th
1994	6th
1995	1st
1996	2nd
1997	2nd
1998	9th
1999	1st
2000	1st
2001	1st

people?" By entering the race, he not only discovered who they were, but also who he was — a winner regardless of where he placed.

Says fellow pilot Jay Hudson of Talkeetna about Bowers's passion for the Iditarod, "Oh, it was everything to him."

Montana musher **Doug Swingley**, the only non-Alaskan Iditarod winner, currently holds the title as champion, leading the pack for three years straight. He has run the race every March since 1992, winning it for the first time in 1995, and consistently placing in the top 10. In 2000, Swingley beat his own record and set a new one, finishing the race in nine days, 58 minutes, six seconds, slightly less than half the time it took the 1973 front-runner to reach Nome.

The 2002 race, he predicts, will "unfortunately be the same people, dominated by the same characters." His list includes himself. "I'd love to see DeeDee [Jonrowe] or someone new win — not that I don't want to win," he says, "but guys like me, Buser, Swenson, King, we've won enough that it's not that exciting anymore. I enjoy seeing the new guys coming up."

"Just being out there" is Swingley's favorite aspect of the Iditarod. He calls running it a "chance of a lifetime," and thrives on the silence and solitude of the trail. "You see lots of northern lights," he says, "lots of caribou and moose." The Elim checkpoint is always a welcome sight for Swingley, who begins to relax at that point in the race. Getting back into the trees after crossing windblown Norton Sound, a frozen, barren expanse more than 50 miles across, he knows he's not far from the finish line.

Swingley lives on a ranch in the Rocky Mountains 5,600 feet above sea level, several thousand feet higher than where Alaskans train their teams, leading some to think his dogs gain an advantage from the decrease in altitude when racing the Iditarod. Swingley, however, attributes his success to a rigorous training schedule and to breeding dogs that physically and mentally thrive on distance racing. "I let the dogs run loose a lot," he says of the 80 canines that share his land. □

Bibliography

Attla, George. *The Iditarod: the Most Demanding Race of All.* As told to and edited by Bella Levorsen. Rome, NY: Arner Publications, 1974.

Bowers, Don. *Back of the Pack: An Iditarod Rookie Musher's Alaska Pilgrimage to Nome.* Foreword by Martin Buser. Anchorage: Publication Consultants, 1998.

Brown, Tricia. *Iditarod Country: Exploring the Route of The Last Great Race®.* Photographs by Jeff Schultz. Seattle: Epicenter Press, 1998.

Cadwallader, Charles Lee. *Reminiscences of the Iditarod Trail: Placer Mining Days in Alaska.* N.p., n.d.

Carter, M[arilyn]. *Iditarod Trail: The Old and the New.* Palmer, Alaska: Aladdin, 1990.

Cole, Terrence, ed. *Nome: "City of the Golden Beaches."* Vol. 11, no. 1. Series editor Robert A. Henning. Anchorage: Alaska Geographic Society, 1984.

Coppinger, Lorna. *The World of Sled Dogs: From Siberia to Sport Racing.* 5th ed. New York: Howell Book House, 1987.

Coppinger, Raymond, and Lorna Coppinger. *Dogs: A Startling New Understanding of Canine Origin, Behavior, and Evolution.* New York: Scribner, 2001.

Couch, James S. *Philately Below Zero: A Postal History of Alaska.* State College, Pa.: The American Philatelic Society, 1957.

Dolan, Ellen M. *Susan Butcher and the Iditarod Trail.* New York: Walker, 1993.

Ensminger, M.E. *The Complete Book of Dogs.* South Brunswick and New York: A.S. Barnes and Company, 1977.

Flanders, Noel K. *The Joy of Running Sled Dogs: A Step-by-Step Guide.* Loveland, Colo.: Alpine, 1989.

Freedman, Lew. *Father of the Iditarod: The Joe Redington Story.* Fairbanks: Epicenter Press, 1999.
—, compiler. *Iditarod Classics: Tales of the Trail From the Men and Women Who Race Across Alaska.* Fairbanks: Epicenter Press, 1992.
—. *Iditarod Silver.* Photographs by Jeff Schultz. Fairbanks: Epicenter Press, 1997.
—, and DeeDee Jonrowe. *Iditarod Dreams: A year in the life of Alaskan sled dog racer DeeDee Jonrowe.* Fairbanks: Epicenter Press, 1995.

Gideon, Kenneth. *Wandering Boy: Alaska — 1913 to 1918.* Fairfax, Va.: East Publishing Co., 1967.

Gill, Shelley. *Iditarod: The Last Great Race to Nome. The Official Iditarod Curriculum Teaching Guide.* Illustrated by Shannon Cartwright. Homer, Alaska: Paws IV, 1993.

Heacox, Kim. *Iditarod Spirit.* Foreword by Joe Redington Sr. Drawings by Donna Gates-King. Portland: Graphic Arts Center, 1991.

Hood, Mary H. *A Fan's Guide to the Iditarod.* Loveland, Colo.: Alpine Blue Ribbon Books, 1996.

Jones, Tim. *The Last Great Race.* Seattle: Madrona Publishers, 1982.

Mackey, Billy E. *Iditarod: Portrait of an Alaska Gold Rush Community.* Ann Arbor: UMI Dissertation Services, 1989.

Mattson, Sue, ed. *Iditarod Fact Book: A Complete Guide to the Last Great Race®.* Illustrated by Jon Van Zyle. Photographs by Jeff Schultz. Research by Andrea Bachhuber. Kenmore, Wash.: Epicenter Press, 2001.

Mattson, Ted. *Adventures of the Iditarod Air Force: True Stories about the Pilots Who Fly for Alaska's Famous Sled Dog Race.* Illustrated by Sandy Jamieson. Fairbanks: Epicenter Press, 1997.

Nielsen, Nicki J. *The Iditarod: Women on the Trail.* Anchorage: Wolfdog, 1986.

O'Donoghue, Brian Patrick. *Honest Dogs: A Story of Triumph and Regret from the World's Toughest Sled Dog Race.* N.p.: Epicenter Press, 1999.
—. *My Lead Dog Was a Lesbian: Mushing Across Alaska in the Iditarod – the World's Most Grueling Race.* New York: Random House, Vintage Books, Vintage Departures, 1996.

Page, Dorothy, ed. *Iditarod Trail Annual.* 1974 to 1989. N.p.

Pitcher, James S. *Sourdough Jim Pitcher: The Autobiography of a Pioneer Alaskan.* Foreword by Ethel Dassow. Anchorage: Alaska Northwest Publishing, 1985.

Rennick, Penny, ed. *Dogs of the North.* Vol. 14, no. 1. Anchorage: Alaska Geographic Society, 1987.

Riddles, Libby. *Storm Run.* Illustrated by Shannon Cartwright. Homer, Alaska.: Paws IV, 1996.
——, and Tim Jones. *Race Across Alaska: First woman to win the Iditarod tells her story.* Harrisburg: Stackpole Books, 1988.

Sherwonit, Bill. *Iditarod: The Great Race to Nome.* Photographs by Jeff Schultz. Foreword by Joe Redington Sr. Preface by Susan Butcher. Anchorage: Alaska Northwest Books, 1991.

Shields, Mary. *Sled Dog Trails.* Illustrated by Nancy van Veenan. Anchorage: Alaska Northwest Publishing, 1984.

Swenson, Rick, with Steve Chamberlain. *The Secrets of Long Distance Training and Racing.* N.p.,1987.

Ungermann, Kenneth A. *The Race to Nome: The story of the heroic Alaskan dog teams that rushed diphtheria serum to stricken Nome in 1925.* Edited by Walter Lord. New York: Harper and Row, 1963.

U.S. Department of the Interior, Bureau of Land Management. *The Iditarod National Historic Trail Seward to Nome Route: A Comprehensive Management Plan.* Anchorage: Bureau of Land Management, Anchorage District Office, 1986.
—, Bureau of Outdoor Recreation. *The Iditarod Trail (Seward-Nome Route) and Other Alaskan Gold Rush Trails.* N.p., 1977.

Wood, Ted. *Iditarod Dreams: Dusty and His Sled Dogs Compete in Alaska's Jr. Iditarod.* New York: Walker, 1996.

www.adn.com/iditarod (Anchorage Daily News)
www.ak.blm.gov/ado/inhthome.html (Bureau of Land Management)
www.cabelasiditarod.com (Cabela's Iditarod Trail Sled Dog Race Coverage)
www.iditarod.com (Iditarod Trail Committee)
www.iditasport.com (Iditasport)
www.nomekennelclub.com (Nome Kennel Club)
www.ptialaska.net/~pride1/ (Mush with P.R.I.D.E.) ■

Index

STATEMENT OF OWNERSHIP, MANAGEMENT AND CIRCULATION

ALASKA GEOGRAPHIC® is a quarterly publication, home office at P.O. Box 93370, Anchorage, AK 99509. Editor is Penny Rennick. Publisher and owner is The Alaska Geographic Society, a non-profit Alaska organization, P.O. Box 93370, Anchorage AK 99509. *ALASKA GEOGRAPHIC*® has a membership of 3889.

Total number of copies 8249

Paid and/or requested circulation
    Sales through dealers, etc. 0
    Mail subscription 3941
Total paid and/or requested circulation 3941
Free distribution 100
Total distribution 4041
Copies not distributed (office use, returns, etc.) 4208

Total 8249

I certify that the statement above is correct and complete.

—Kathy Doogan, Co-Chair, Alaska Geographic Society

ALASKA GEOGRAPHIC. Back Issues

Membership in The Alaska Geographic Society includes a subscription to *ALASKA GEOGRAPHIC®*, the Society's colorful, award-winning quarterly. Contact us for current membership rates or to request a free catalog.

The *ALASKA GEOGRAPHIC®* back issues listed below can be ordered directly from us. **NOTE:** This list was current in late 2001. If more than a year has elapsed since that time, be sure to contact us before ordering to check prices and availability of back issues, particularly for books marked "Limited."

When ordering back issues please add shipping: $5 for the first book and $2 for each additional book. Inquire for shipping rates to non-U.S. addresses. To order, send check or money order (U.S. funds) or VISA or MasterCard information (including expiration date and daytime phone number) with list of titles desired to:

ALASKA GEOGRAPHIC.

P.O. Box 93370 • Anchorage, AK 99509-3370
Phone (907) 562-0164 • Toll free (888) 255-6697
Fax (907) 562-0479 • e-mail: info@akgeo.com

The North Slope, Vol. 1, No. 1. Out of print.
One Man's Wilderness, Vol. 1, No. 2. Out of print.
Admiralty...Island in Contention, Vol. 1, No. 3. $9.95.
Fisheries of the North Pacific, Vol. 1, No. 4. Out of print.
Alaska-Yukon Wild Flowers, Vol. 2, No. 1. Out of print.
Richard Harrington's Yukon, Vol. 2, No. 2. Out of print.
Prince William Sound, Vol. 2, No. 3. Out of print.
Yakutat: The Turbulent Crescent, Vol. 2, No. 4. Out of print.
Glacier Bay: Old Ice, New Land, Vol. 3, No. 1. Out of print.
The Land: Eye of the Storm, Vol. 3, No. 2. Out of print.
Richard Harrington's Antarctic, Vol. 3, No. 3. $9.95.
The Silver Years, Vol. 3, No. 4. $21.95. Limited.
Alaska's Volcanoes, Vol. 4, No. 1. Out of print.
The Brooks Range, Vol. 4, No. 2. Out of print.
Kodiak: Island of Change, Vol. 4, No. 3. Out of print.
Wilderness Proposals, Vol. 4, No. 4. Out of print.
Cook Inlet Country, Vol. 5, No. 1. Out of print.
Southeast: Alaska's Panhandle, Vol. 5, No. 2. Out of print.
Bristol Bay Basin, Vol. 5, No. 3. Out of print.
Alaska Whales and Whaling, Vol. 5, No. 4. $19.95.
Yukon-Kuskokwim Delta, Vol. 6, No. 1. Out of print.
Aurora Borealis, Vol. 6, No. 2. $21.95. Limited
Alaska's Native People, Vol. 6, No. 3. $29.95. Limited.
The Stikine River, Vol. 6, No. 4. $9.95.
Alaska's Great Interior, Vol. 7, No. 1. $19.95.
Photographic Geography of Alaska, Vol. 7, No. 2. Out of print.
The Aleutians, Vol. 7, No. 3. Out of print.

Klondike Lost, Vol. 7, No. 4. Out of print.
Wrangell-Saint Elias, Vol. 8, No. 1. Out of print.
Alaska Mammals, Vol. 8, No. 2. Out of print.
The Kotzebue Basin, Vol. 8, No. 3. Out of print.
Alaska National Interest Lands, Vol. 8, No. 4. $19.95.
*Alaska's Glaciers, Vol. 9, No. 1. Rev. 1993. $21.95. Limited.
Sitka and Its Ocean/Island World, Vol. 9, No. 2. Out of print.
Islands of the Seals: The Pribilofs, Vol. 9, No. 3. $9.95.
Alaska's Oil/Gas & Minerals Industry, Vol. 9, No. 4. $9.95.
Adventure Roads North, Vol. 10, No. 1. $9.95.
Anchorage and the Cook Inlet Basin, Vol. 10, No. 2. $19.95.
Alaska's Salmon Fisheries, Vol. 10, No. 3. $9.95.
Up the Koyukuk, Vol. 10, No. 4. $9.95.
Nome: City of Golden Beaches, Vol. 11, No. 1. $21.95. Limited.
Alaska's Farms and Gardens, Vol. 11, No. 2. $19.95.
Chilkat River Valley, Vol. 11, No. 3. $9.95.
Alaska Steam, Vol. 11, No. 4. $19.95.
Northwest Territories, Vol. 12, No. 1. $9.95.
Alaska's Forest Resources, Vol. 12, No. 2. $9.95.
Alaska Native Arts and Crafts, Vol. 12, No. 3. $24.95.
Our Arctic Year, Vol. 12, No. 4. $19.95.
* Where Mountains Meet the Sea, Vol. 13, No. 1. $19.95.
Backcountry Alaska, Vol. 13, No. 2. $9.95.
British Columbia's Coast, Vol. 13, No. 3. $9.95.
Lake Clark/Lake Iliamna, Vol. 13, No. 4. Out of print.
Dogs of the North, Vol. 14, No. 1. Out of print.
South/Southeast Alaska, Vol. 14, No. 2. $21.95. Limited.
Alaska's Seward Peninsula, Vol. 14, No. 3. $19.95.
The Upper Yukon Basin, Vol. 14, No. 4. $19.95.
Glacier Bay: Icy Wilderness, Vol. 15, No. 1. Out of print.
Dawson City, Vol. 15, No. 2. $19.95.
Denali, Vol. 15, No. 3. $9.95.
The Kuskokwim River, Vol. 15, No. 4. $19.95.
Katmai Country, Vol. 16, No. 1. $19.95.
North Slope Now, Vol. 16, No. 2. $9.95.
The Tanana Basin, Vol. 16, No. 3. $9.95.
* The Copper Trail, Vol. 16, No. 4. $19.95.
* The Nushagak Basin, Vol. 17, No. 1. $19.95.
* Juneau, Vol. 17, No. 2. Out of print.
* The Middle Yukon River, Vol. 17, No. 3. $19.95.
* The Lower Yukon River, Vol. 17, No. 4. $19.95.
* Alaska's Weather, Vol. 18, No. 1. $9.95.
* Alaska's Volcanoes, Vol. 18, No. 2. $19.95.
* Admiralty Island: Fortress of Bears, Vol. 18, No. 3. Out of print.
Unalaska/Dutch Harbor, Vol. 18, No. 4. Out of print.
* Skagway: A Legacy of Gold, Vol. 19, No. 1. $9.95.
Alaska: The Great Land, Vol. 19, No. 2. $9.95.
Kodiak, Vol. 19, No. 3. Out of print.
Alaska's Railroads, Vol. 19, No. 4. $19.95.
Prince William Sound, Vol. 20, No. 1. $9.95.
Southeast Alaska, Vol. 20, No. 2. $19.95.
Arctic National Wildlife Refuge, Vol. 20, No. 3. $19.95.
Alaska's Bears, Vol. 20, No. 4. $19.95.

The Alaska Peninsula, Vol. 21, No. 1. $19.95.
The Kenai Peninsula, Vol. 21, No. 2. $19.95.
People of Alaska, Vol. 21, No. 3. $19.95.
Prehistoric Alaska, Vol. 21, No. 4. $19.95.
Fairbanks, Vol. 22, No. 1. $19.95.
The Aleutian Islands, Vol. 22, No. 2. $19.95.
Rich Earth: Alaska's Mineral Industry, Vol. 22, No. 3. $19.95.
World War II in Alaska, Vol. 22, No. 4. $19.95.
Anchorage, Vol. 23, No. 1. $21.95.
Native Cultures in Alaska, Vol. 23, No. 2. $19.95.
The Brooks Range, Vol. 23, No. 3. $19.95.
Moose, Caribou and Muskox, Vol. 23, No. 4. $19.95.
Alaska's Southern Panhandle, Vol. 24, No. 1. $19.95.
The Golden Gamble, Vol. 24, No. 2. $19.95.
Commercial Fishing in Alaska, Vol. 24, No. 3. $19.95.
Alaska's Magnificent Eagles, Vol. 24, No. 4. $19.95.
Steve McCutcheon's Alaska, Vol. 25, No. 1. $21.95.
Yukon Territory, Vol. 25, No. 2. $21.95.
Climbing Alaska, Vol. 25, No. 3. $21.95.
Frontier Flight, Vol. 25, No. 4. $21.95.
Restoring Alaska: Legacy of an Oil Spill, Vol. 26, No. 1. $21.95.
World Heritage Wilderness, Vol. 26, No. 2. $21.95.
The Bering Sea, Vol. 26, No. 3. $21.95.
Russian America, Vol. 26, No. 4, $21.95
Best of *ALASKA GEOGRAPHIC®*, Vol. 27, No. 1, $24.95
Seals, Sea Lions and Sea Otters, Vol. 27, No. 2, $21.95
Painting Alaska, Vol. 27, No. 3, $21.95
Living Off the Land, Vol. 27, No. 4, $21.95
Exploring Alaska's Birds, Vol. 28, No. 1, $23.95
Glaciers of Alaska, Vol. 28, No. 2, $23.95
Inupiaq and Yupik People of Alaska, Vol. 28, No. 3, $23.95

* **Available in hardback (library binding) — $24.95 each.**

PRICES AND AVAILABILITY SUBJECT TO CHANGE

NEXT ISSUE: Vol. 29, No. 1

Secrets of the Aurora Borealis

The dazzling northern lights shine in this all-new book by aurora experts at the International Arctic Research Center. Find out what makes the sky dance, why scientists study the aurora, the latest discoveries, and the best places to see this mesmerizing display. Excellent photos offer an intriguing look at the aurora and at the science behind the magical lights. To members spring 2002.